All the Dates

The official day-by-day history of Sunderland AFC

Compiled by Mike Gibson

Edited by Rob Mason

First published in the United Kingdom in 2009 by Ignition Publications Limited, Hawk Creative Business Park, Easingwold, York, YO61 3FE.

Copyright © Sunderland AFC, 2009

All Rights Reserved. No part of this publication may be reproduced, stored in a retrieval system, or transmitted in any form or by any means, electronic, mechanical, photocopying or otherwise without the prior permission in writing of the copywright holders, nor be circulated in any other form or binding or cover other than in which it is published and without a similar condition being imposed on the subsequent publisher.

Photographs supplied by Getty Images and PA Photos and are reproduced under licence as an official publication of Sunderland AFC produced by Ignition Publications Limited. Additional imagery supplied from the author's collection.

ISBN 978-0-9562703-0-6

Origination and design by Trevor Hartley for Ignition Publications Limited.
Printed and bound in the United Kingdom.

All The Dates is an official Sunderland AFC publication.

Mike Gibson at The Amsterdam Tournament, 2009

INTRODUCTION

When is your birthday? How about your mam or dad's birthday? Whatever days in the calendar are important to you and your family 'All the Dates' will give you an at a glance guide as to why those dates are important to Sunderland AFC.

Mike Gibson has compiled four facts from every day of the year – including February 29th and right through the summer months.

Great games, significant moments, dates of transfers, births and deaths of special players and managers are listed in this official SAFC book, which is intended to be a companion volume to the excellent 'All the Lads' by Garth Dykes and Doug Lamming which provided a biography of every player to ever play first team football for Sunderland. Mike Gibson has twice updated 'All the Lads' in Sunderland's official match programme 'Red and White' where he is a regular and respected contributor.

Born and brought up in Sunderland, Mike Gibson worked with fellow 'Red and White' contributor Barry Jackson and Sunderland AFC Publications Officer Rob Mason to produce 'Sunderland the Complete Record' in 2005.

JANUARY

JANUARY 1

2007 Sunderland won their first New Year's Day game since 1915 thanks to goals from Hysen and Connolly at Leicester City. This was the start of a record 17 League game unbeaten run from the start of a calendar year.
(see April 21st)

2001 Julio Arca's sublime free kick sparked a Sunderland recovery after going behind at home to Ipswich Town. This 4-1 win moved The Lads into third place in the Premiership.

1955 A first half goal from Ken Chisholm earned the Black Cats a 1-1 draw at home to Spurs and consolidated their place at the top of Division One.

1953 Sunderland and Aston Villa became the first English clubs to meet in 100 League games.

JANUARY 2

2006 Liam Lawrence became the first Sunderland player to win BBC TV's Match of the Day Goal of the Month competition with a stunning left foot volley from the edge of the penalty area in The Lads' 2-1 defeat at Fulham.

1999 Martin Scott was stretchered off with an ankle injury in what turned out to be his final game; third round FA Cup tie at Lincoln City.

1978 Roly Gregoire became the first black player to play for Sunderland when he made his debut in a 2-0 home victory over Hull City.

1895 Sunderland drew 4-4 with Aston Villa at Newcastle Road ground. This was captured in oils by Thomas Hemy, is thought to be the oldest football painting in the world and hangs in the entrance to The Stadium of Light.

JANUARY 3

1998 Kevin Phillips scored four goals at Rotherham in a 5-1 third round FA Cup victory. This was Sunderland's 300th game in this competition.

1988 Birth of Sunderland Young Player of the Year in 2006-07 and 2007-08, Jonny Evans, in Belfast.

1953 A Trevor Ford penalty and goals from Len Shackleton and Billy Bingham secured a 3-1 home win over Arsenal that put Sunderland on top of Division One.

1885 Sunderland suffered their worst defeat in any game; 11-1 at home to Port Glasgow in a friendly.

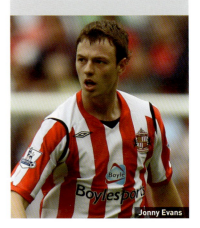
Jonny Evans

JANUARY 4

1992 Death of Scottish international forward Patrick Gallacher aged 82.

1986 Sunderland beat Newport County, their 100th different first team opposition, 2-0 in a third round FA Cup tie thanks to George Burley's and David Corner's first goals for The Lads.

1955 Charlie Fleming signed from East Fife for £7,000 plus Tommy Wright moving in the opposite direction.

1902 The Black Cats remained top of Division One following a 3-0 win at Manchester City.

JANUARY 5

1980 Sunderland suffered their only home defeat (1-0) during 1979-80; against First Division Bolton Wanderers in a third round FA Cup tie.

1970 Death of David Halliday aged 68; Sunderland's record goalscorer in one season. (43 in 1928-29)

1957 The Lads easily progressed to the FA Cup fourth round with a 4-0 home win over Third Division (South) side Queens Park Rangers.

1946 Sunderland resumed first team football after WW2 at Grimsby Town in their first ever two legged FA Cup tie.

JANUARY 6

2001 Stan Varga became the 100th Sunderland player to be sent off in competitive fixtures when he received a red card in the goalless FA Cup third round home tie with Crystal Palace.

1996 Division One Sunderland drew 2-2 at Premiership Manchester United after a late equaliser by Eric Cantona.

1973 Bob Stokoe recorded his first home win; a 4-0 victory over Brighton & Hove Albion. This game also saw Joe Bolton's first strike for The Lads.

1912 Five second half goals, including a brace each for Holley and Mordue, gave Sunderland a 5-0 home win over Notts County.

JANUARY 7

1985 Death of Sunderland's only full English international goalkeeper Albert McInroy aged 83.

1967 George Herd became the first Sunderland substitute to score when he netted the second half equaliser in a 1-1 draw at Blackpool.

1957 A story was published in newspapers stating that Sunderland were paying additional payments to players in excess of the maximum wage. The anonymous letter was written by Mr Smith. (see April 10th, April 25th & May 17th)

1862 Birth of John Auld in Lugar, Ayrshire; Sunderland's first captain after becoming a League club in 1890.

06.01.1996 An FA Cup draw at Old Trafford

JANUARY 8

2005 A 2-1 third round FA Cup win over Premiership Crystal Palace marked The Lads 100th win in all competitions at the Stadium of Light.

2000 Clint Hill of Tranmere Rovers was sent off in the final minute of a fourth round FA Cup tie against Sunderland at Prenton Park. However in the confusion the referee allowed Stephen Frail to replace him as a substitute thus maintaining Tranmere's eleven.

1968 Former England forward Gordon Harris was signed from Burnley for £68,000.

1938 Sunderland's route to their second successive FA Cup semi final began with a 1-0 home win over Watford courtesy of a first half Len Duns strike. The next three rounds also ended in 1-0 Sunderland victories.

JANUARY 9

1999 A last minute Niall Quinn header rescued a point for Sunderland in a 2-2 draw at Queens Park Rangers.

1974 FA Cup holders Sunderland lost 1-0 to Carlisle United in a third round FA Cup replay at Roker Park.

1926 Sunderland beat Boston 8-1 in a third round FA Cup tie with Bob Kelly and David Halliday both getting hat tricks.

1904 Renowned Edwardian film makers Mitchell and Kenyon recorded what is believed to be the oldest footage of Sunderland; taken at Roker Park in a league game against Middlesbrough.

JANUARY 10

2003 Estonian international goalkeeper Mart Poom signed from Derby County for £2 million following a loan spell from November 17th.

1979 A Gary Rowell penalty and a goal from Bob Lee gave Sunderland a 2-1 victory in a third round FA Cup tie over top flight opposition, Everton, on a snowy evening at Roker Park.

1914 Sunderland beat Chatham Town 9-0 in a first round FA Cup tie with James Richardson netting his second four goal haul for The Lads.

1891 John Campbell scored the first home League hat trick by a Sunderland player; v Aston Villa in a 5-1 victory.

JANUARY 11

2003 A goalless draw at home to Blackburn Rovers ultimately proved to be the last point recorded that season as the remaining fifteen Premiership games all ended in defeats.

1992 A Don Goodman hat trick in fifteen second half minutes helped Sunderland convert a 1-1 half time score into a 6-2 home victory against Millwall.

1986 Nick Pickering scored a hat trick at Roker Park in a 4-2 victory over Leeds United in his penultimate League appearance for The Lads. (see January 25th)

1913 Sunderland beat Clapton Orient 6-0 in a first round FA Cup tie with James Richardson scoring four of the goals.

09.01.99 Niall Quinn

JANUARY 12

1985 Reuben Agboola's debut was expunged from the record books as the game against Liverpool at Roker Park was abandoned at half time due to a frozen pitch with score at 0-0.

1963 Sunderland appeared in their first League Cup semi final losing 3-1 at Roker Park against Aston Villa in the first of two legs. (see April 23rd)

1937 Full back Bill Murray was transferred to St Mirren after 328 games for Sunderland. He returned as manager a little over two years later. (see March 24th)

1901 The Black Cats moved into second place in the top flight with a 7-2 win over Wolverhampton Wanderers at Roker Park.

JANUARY 13

2007 £2 million signing Anthony Stokes made his debut against Ipswich Town in a 1-0 home victory.

1973 Centre half Dave Watson grabbed a late equaliser at Notts County to earn a third round FA Cup replay in the first of the games that ultimately led to triumph over Leeds United in the final. (see May 5th)

1962 James O'Neill scored two goals on his debut against Bristol Rovers in a 6-1 victory.

1932 Former England centre forward Harry Bedford signed from Newcastle United for £3,000.

JANUARY 14

2003 Midfielders Sean Thornton and Nicolas Medina made their debuts against Bolton Wanderers in a third round FA Cup replay; the first FA Cup replay to be staged at the Stadium of Light.

1978 Gary Rowell missed his only first team penalty for Sunderland out of the twenty six he took. He put the ball wide of the post at Brisbane Road against Orient. Central defender Rob Hindmarch became Sunderland's second youngest defender, behind Cec Irwin, aged 16 years 262 days. (see September 20th)

1947 Full back Arthur Hudgell signed from Crystal Palace for £7,500.

1894 Birth of Sunderland's oldest ever ex-player, Joe Kasher, in Willington. He died six days before his 98th birthday.

13.01.07 Anthony Stokes

JANUARY 15

1997 Sunderland lost 2-0 against Arsenal in Roker Park's last ever FA Cup tie. (third round replay)

1973 FA Cup winning left back Ron Guthrie was signed from Newcastle United for £15,000 by Bob Stokoe.

1927 David Halliday scored his third of four hat tricks that season as The Lads recorded a 4-1 win over West Bromwich Albion at Roker Park.

1903 Arthur Bridgett signed from Stoke; the only Sunderland player ever to refuse to play on religious days; his reason being that he was an active member of The Brotherhood Movement.

Arthur Bridgett

JANUARY 24

2004 Simon Ramsden came on as a 90th minute substitute, v Ipswich Town, for his only first team appearance. The two minutes of injury time he played gave him the shortest career of any Sunderland player.
1990 Paul Lemon played his final game and Gary Owers was sent off in a 5-0 fifth round League Cup replay defeat at Coventry City.
1931 Thomas Urwin became the first Sunderland player to be sent off in an FA Cup tie; in a fourth round draw at Bolton.
1914 Sunderland consolidated second place in Division One with a 4-2 home win over Middlesbrough.

JANUARY 25

2007 Right back Danny Simpson signed on loan from Manchester United. He played fourteen games for The Lads and never appeared on the losing side.
1986 Nick Pickering played his final game for Sunderland; a goalless fourth round FA Cup tie at home to Manchester United.
1964 Sunderland beat Bristol City 6-1 in a fourth round FA Cup tie thanks to goals from Herd (2), Hurley, Sharkey and Crossan (2).
1899 Long serving forward William Farquhar signed from Elgin City.

Danny Simpson

JANUARY 26

1998 Striker Danny Dichio moved from Sampdoria to Sunderland for £750,000.
1995 Death of ex-left back Jack Jones aged 81. He was on the Roker Park staff as player then assistant trainer from 1945 to 1968.
1958 Birth of England `B' international Shaun Elliott in Hayden Bridge.
1895 Prolific Victorian era forwards Campbell and Millar were amongst the goals in a 5-2 win at Stoke that kept the "Team of all the Talents" top of Division One.

Danny Dichio

JANUARY 27

2004 Castletown born Michael Gray transferred to Blackburn Rovers after almost fourteen years on Sunderland's books.
1973 Scottish international striker John Hughes suffered a career ending knee injury in his only game for Sunderland. Brother Billy also played in this game against Millwall at Roker Park.
1951 Sunderland played in a borrowed set of Newcastle United home shirts for their fourth round home FA Cup tie due to a colour clash with opponents Southampton.
1934 The Lads suffered one of their worst FA Cup defeats; 7-2 at Aston Villa. This proved to be Jock McDougall's and Benny Yorston's final game for Sunderland.

JANUARY 28

2002 Swedish international defender Joachim Bjorklund signed from Venezia for £1.5 million.

1981 Sunderland beat Manchester United 2-0 in a Wednesday night re-arranged League game. Goals from Gordon Chisholm and Gary Rowell (penalty) secured the points on Ian Bowyer's debut.

1979 **Birth of Jeff Whitley in Ndola, the same Zambian birthplace as former goalkeeper Iain Hesford.**

1933 Bobby Gurney scored a hat trick in a 3-0 FA Cup third round win at Villa Park in front of almost 54,000 fans.

Joachim Bjorklund

JANUARY 29

2007 Trinidad and Tobago international striker Stern John signed from Coventry City for an undisclosed fee.

1995 Phil Gray scored Sunderland's 500th FA Cup goal in the televised 4-1 home defeat by Tottenham Hotspur and Gary Bennett set an unwanted Club record with his fifth red card.

1964 Birth of right back John Kay in Sunderland.

1949 Sunderland lost 2-1, after extra time, at non-League Yeovil Town in a fourth round FA Cup tie. This was left back Bernard Ramsden's final game for The Lads.

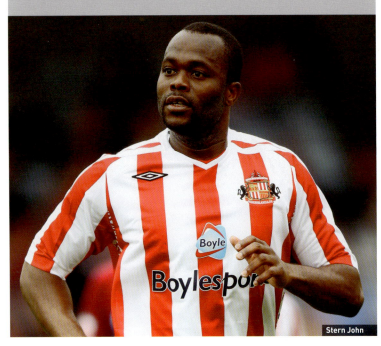

Stern John

JANUARY 30

1999 Sunderland lost 2-1 at Watford but then went on an unbeaten League run of 14 wins and 3 draws for the remainder of the season.

1988 A 2-1 victory over Gillingham moved Sunderland four points clear at the top of Division Three.

1935 Sunderland lost 6-4 after extra time at Everton in a fourth round FA Cup replay.

1932 Benny Yorston scored on his debut v Blackpool. He went on to score in seven of his first eight games for The Lads.

31.01.2001

JANUARY 31

2004 First game to be postponed at The Stadium of Light; v Preston North End due to a waterlogged pitch.

2001 Michael Gray and Alex Rae were sent off, along with Andy Cole, in a 1-0 televised home defeat by Manchester United. It was second placed Sunderland's first home defeat of the season.

1949 Ivor Broadis became the first manager to transfer himself when as player manager of Carlisle United he moved to Sunderland for £19,000.

1918 Death of former centre half Sandy McAllister from Bright's Disease whilst serving with the Northumberland Fusiliers in Italy.

FEBRUARY

FEBRUARY 1

2004 Death of former manager Bob Stokoe aged 73. "The Messiah" was twice in charge (1972 to 1976 & as caretaker manager in 1987) and famously led the Club to FA Cup glory in 1973.

2003 Stephen Wright and Michael Proctor (2) scored own goals within the space of eight first half minutes at home to Charlton Athletic.

1993 Malcolm Crosby sacked as manager. Bobby Ferguson took over as caretaker manager for four days until Terry Butcher was appointed as Sunderland's first full-time player manager.

1913 The FA Cup second round tie at Hyde Road against Manchester City was abandoned after 60 minutes due to a crowd invasion with Sunderland leading 2-0.

FEBRUARY 2

1985 David Hodgson headed Sunderland's only goal, past former Black Cat Barry Siddall, in a 1-0 home win over bottom club Stoke City.

1955 Birth of hard tackling left back Joe Bolton in Birtley.

1920 Birth of George Hardwick in Saltburn who was Sunderland's manager during the 1964-65 season.

1895 Sunderland recorded their record first team victory, 11-1, with Jimmy Millar netting five, in a first round FA Cup tie, at home to Manchester based Fairfield. It is the only occasion that The Lads have scored at least five goals in each half and was in front of their lowest FA Cup attendance; an estimated 1,500 people.

FEBRUARY 3

2007 Trinidad & Tobago forward Stern John made his debut against his former club, Coventry City. Full back Danny Simpson, on loan from Manchester United, also made his debut, coming on as a late second half substitute.

1973 Charlie Hurley returned to Roker Park for the first time as a manager, with Reading in a fourth round FA Cup tie, and received a standing ovation when walking to the dugout.

1927 "Prince of Fullbacks" Warney Cresswell transferred to Everton for £7,000 after 190 first team appearances.

1901 Birth of Ernie England in Shirebrook, Nottinghamshire. He holds the record for most appearances (352) for a Sunderland outfield player without scoring.

Bob Stokoe

FEBRUARY 4

1984 Craig Russell was Sunderland's mascot at home to Liverpool on his tenth birthday.

1948 "Clown Prince of Soccer" Leonard Francis Shackleton signed from Newcastle United for a British record fee of £20,050.

1931 Joe Devine scored on his debut in an 8-2 victory over Blackburn Rovers. Sunderland led 7-0 at half time; their best ever opening forty five minutes performance.

1904 Andrew McCombie transferred to Newcastle United for a record fee of £700.

FEBRUARY 5

2003 Sunderland settled an FA Cup tie for the first time by a penalty shoot out after their fourth round FA Cup replay against Blackburn Rovers ended 2-2. Kevin Phillips, in netting the first goal, became Sunderland's highest post WW2 scorer in FA Cup ties with ten.

1936 Goalkeeper Jimmy Thorpe died in hospital, aged 22, after being in a diabetic coma as a result of injuries sustained during the game against Chelsea on 1st February. His 1935-36 League Championship medal was later presented to his widow.

1907 Death of former "Team of all the Talents" forward Jimmy Millar aged 36 from tuberculosis whilst trainer at Chelsea.

1896 Birth of Thomas Urwin in Haswell, County Durham; the only player to receive a benefit from all three major north east clubs and also Sunderland's oldest player. (see April 22nd)

FEBRUARY 6

2004 Sunderland born Michael Proctor transferred to Rotherham United in a swap deal for Darren Byfield.

1993 Gordon Armstrong and Kevin Ball both fail from the penalty spot as Terry Butcher's first game in charge ended in a 1-0 home defeat at the hands of Swindon Town.

1954 The Black Cats recorded their third successive victory, the best run in a disappointing season. Goals from Billy Elliott, Len Shackleton and Ted Purdon, his sixth in three games, secured a 3-1 win over Portsmouth at Roker.

1936 Death of Charles Bellany Thomson, Sunderland's 1913 FA Cup Final captain and centre half, aged 57.

05.02.03 Kevin Phillips scores his penalty in the shoot-out with Blackburn.

FEBRUARY 7

1998 Midfielder Chris Lumsdon made his debut, and only appearance that season, and Gareth Hall made his final appearance in a 1-0 away victory at Molineux.

1973 FA Cup winning striker Vic Halom signed from Luton Town for £35,000.

1959 Birth of ex-manager Mick McCarthy in Barnsley.

1906 Sunderland paid Gainsborough Trinity £300 to switch the FA Cup second round replay to Roker Park as The Lads had a poor away record. The result was a 3-0 victory to Sunderland but a financial loss as the match takings were only £244.

FEBRUARY 8

2003 Brazilian centre back Emerson Thome made his final appearance for The Lads; v Tottenham Hotspur. Sunderland's first Moroccan international, Talal El Karkouri, made his debut in this game.

1983 Left back Alan Kennedy scored his only goals for Sunderland in a 2-2 home draw with Carlisle United. The second strike was from fully 35 yards.

1968 Ian McColl sacked as manager after 125 games in charge at Roker Park.

1958 Sunderland lost 7-1 at Luton Town after 6-2 and 8-2 defeats in the previous two seasons.

Ian McColl

FEBRUARY 9

2008 Sunderland beat Wigan Athletic 2-0 at the Stadium of Light to record their fourth successive top flight home victory by two clear goals. The last time this occurred was the start of the 1935-36 season.

1980 Stan Cummins scored four goals in a 5-0 home win over Burnley in only his 12th game for the Club.

1968 Alan Brown appointed Sunderland manager for the second time. (see July 30th)

1946 Alex Hastings' final game; fifth round FA Cup tie at home to Birmingham City. He received the British Empire Medal in 1981 for services to football following twelve years as President of the South Australian Soccer Association.

09.02.08 Sunderland v Wigan

FEBRUARY 10

2007 Anthony Stokes scored his first goal for Sunderland, at Plymouth Argyle, following his £2 million move from Arsenal.

1996 Debut of 17 year old Michael Bridges as substitute for Phil Gray at home to Port Vale.

1912 First instance of two Sunderland players being selected for an international team when Jackie Mordue and George Holley played for England against Ireland in Dublin. Holley scored in the 6-1 victory.

1894 Record receipts of £960 taken at Newcastle Road ground for FA Cup second round 2-2 draw against Aston Villa.

Anthony Stokes

FEBRUARY 11

1989 A Stuart Rimmer hat trick condemned Sunderland to a 3-0 home defeat against bottom side Walsall who had lost their previous fifteen League games. Ironically the game before this run started was a 2-0 home victory over Sunderland.

1977 Mel Holden ended The Lads' worst League goal drought when he scored the only goal at Roker Park against Bristol City. The barren spell had lasted for 1020 minutes.

1946 Birth of Sunderland's 1973 FA Cup Final goal scorer Ian Porterfield in Dunfermline.

1899 Sunderland lost 2-1 away to Southern League side Tottenham Hotspur in an FA Cup second round tie.

Ian Porterfield

FEBRUARY 12

2005 Marcus Stewart scored a hat trick at The Stadium of Light; v Watford in a 4-2 victory.

1972 A brace from Dennis Tueart and one from Ian Porterfield gave The Lads a 3-0 home victory over Oxford United.

1959 Birth of centre forward Mick Harford in Sunderland who although supported Sunderland always had a knack of scoring against them.

1921 Bobby Marshall and Charlie Buchan each scored twice in a convincing 5-1 victory at Villa Park.

FEBRUARY 13

2002 Patrick Mboma became the first Cameroon born player to sign for Sunderland when he joined on loan from Italian side Parma.

1985 Two Colin West goals gave Sunderland a 2-0 home victory in a Milk Cup semi final first leg game against Chelsea.

1981 Birth of midfielder Liam Miller in Cork.

1946 Cyril Brown played his sixth and final game for The Lads. This is the most appearances by a Sunderland player without making a League appearance as all of these games were in the 1945-46 FA Cup.

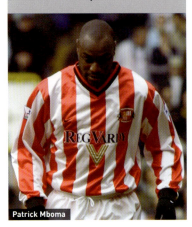
Patrick Mboma

FEBRUARY 14

2004 Division One Sunderland drew 1-1 at home with Premiership Birmingham City in a fifth round FA Cup tie. This game was unusual in recent times as manager Mick McCarthy did not make any substitutions.

1962 Outside left Norman Clarke signed from Ballymena United for £6,000. Clarke shares his middle name with current mascot Samson.

1948 Debut of Len Shackleton in a 5-1 Valentine's Day massacre at Derby County.

1940 Death of Victorian forward John Harvie in Middlesbrough aged 73.

FEBRUARY 15

2003 Sunderland lost 1-0 at home to Watford in a fifth round FA Cup tie through a twice taken Tommy Smith penalty.

1964 Almost 63,000 fans saw The Lads dominate the first half of a fifth round FA Cup tie at home to Everton; going in 3-0 up. The eventual 3-1 victory set up a classic series of games against Manchester United. (see February 29th and March 4th)

1930 Full back Ernie England's final game for The Lads; against Nottingham Forest. (see February 3rd)

1913 Charlie Buchan scored on his England debut against Ireland in Belfast in the only game in which three Sunderland players have appeared for England (Buchan, Mordue & Cuggy). It could have been four if George Holley had not been dropped after playing in the three previous internationals.

Charlie Buchan

FEBRUARY 16

1991 A first half Marco Gabbiadini header at Roker Park gave Sunderland all of the points against Nottingham Forest. This ended his longest goalless spell with the Club.

1957 Len Shackleton became the first Sunderland player to score 100 post WW2 goals when he netted against Sheffield Wednesday. It also turned out to be his final goal for The Lads.

1939 Outside left Jimmy Connor's final game for The Lads; against Blackburn Rovers. His career was effectively cut short due to a cruciate ligament injury.

1905 Inside right Alf Common became the first £1,000 player in Britain when he was transferred to Middlesbrough.

Alf Common

FEBRUARY 17

2007 Sunderland beat Southend United 4-0 to move into a play off place for the first time in that season thanks to goals from Connolly, Hysen and a brace from Stern John.

1998 The Black Cats remained third in Division One with a 4-1 win over Reading; the third successive home game in which they had scored four goals.

1973 Goals from Horswill, Halom, on his home debut, Hughes and Tueart set up a 4-0 victory over Middlesbrough at Roker Park.

1923 Sunderland played their 1000th League game; a goalless draw at Boundary Park against Oldham Athletic.

FEBRUARY 18

1971 Defender Colin Todd moved to Derby County for a Sunderland record fee of £175,000.

1967 A Neil Martin hat trick inspired Sunderland to a 7-1 home demolition of Peterborough United in a fourth round FA Cup tie at Roker Park.

1963 Sunderland beat non-League Gravesend & Northfleet 5-2 in a fourth round FA Cup replay at Roker Park following a 1-1 draw six days earlier in Essex.

1899 England recorded their record victory, 13-2, against Ireland, in the first international to be played at Roker Park. Right back Phil Bach became the second Sunderland player to be capped by England. (see March 7th)

Colin Todd

FEBRUARY 19

1977 Goals from Lee, Holden, Arnott and Rowell secured a 4-0 home win against Middlesbrough in the first of three games that saw The Lads score 16 goals after only netting once in the previous eleven League games. (see February 11th)

1949 Birth of goalkeeper Derek Forster in Newcastle; Sunderland's youngest player at 15 years 185 days. (see August 22nd)

1936 Bobby Gurney scored for the fourth successive game as The Lads beat Grimsby Town 3-1 in a Wednesday afternoon game at Roker.

1870 Birth of centre forward John Campbell in Renton; Sunderland's leading pre-WW1 scorer with 154 goals and recipient of three League Championship medals.

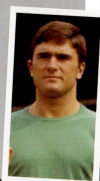
Derek Forster

FEBRUARY 20

1996 Sunderland beat Ipswich Town 1-0, courtesy of a Craig Russell strike, starting a nine game run of maximum points; their best since thirteen consecutive League wins in 1891-92.

1980 Left back Joe Hinnigan signed from Wigan Athletic for £135,000. He never tasted defeat in his first fourteen games as Sunderland achieved promotion to the top flight.

1944 Birth of Ken Knighton in Barnsley; promotion winning Sunderland manager from 1979 to 1981.

1930 Left back Harold Shaw signed from Wolverhampton Wanderers for £7,000.

FEBRUARY 21

1995 A first half goal from Craig Russell gave Sunderland their first win for over nine weeks, 1-0 at Watford, and moved them out of the First Division relegation zone.

1974 Midfielder Denis Longhorn signed from Mansfield Town with John Lathan moving in the opposite direction.

1934 A 6-0 home win over Tottenham Hotspur included Raich Carter's first hat trick for Sunderland.

1921 Sunderland born Barney Travers transferred to Fulham for a British record equalling £3,000.

FEBRUARY 22

2005 Sunderland started a run of eight successive wins with a 4-1 home victory over Rotherham United.

1989 German striker Thomas Hauser signed from Basle Old Boys for £200,000.

1977 Bob Lee bagged a hat trick as the Black Cats continued their sudden goalscoring spree with a 6-1 demolition of West Bromwich Albion. (see February 19th)

1939 Bobby Gurney broke his ankle in the second minute of a fifth round FA Cup second replay against Blackburn Rovers at Hillsborough. This was to be his final appearance for The Lads.

FEBRUARY 23

1980 Current kit manager John Cooke scored his first senior goal for Sunderland in a 1-0 home victory against Luton Town. BBC TV Match of the Day cameras only just captured it as Roker Park was shrouded in fog for much of the game.

1957 6,276 spectators watched England Schoolboys lose 3-2 at Roker Park to Scotland Schoolboys in swirling snow.

1950 Birth of Alan Foggon in Craghead, County Durham, who played for all three of the North East's major clubs plus Hartlepool.

1919 Death of Sunderland's first England international Tom Porteous aged 53. (see March 7th)

FEBRUARY 24

2007 Liam Miller's last minute glancing header sealed a 2-1 home victory against table topping Derby County.

1990 Paul Thirlwell and his brother were mascots for Sunderland in the home game against Brighton & Hove Albion.

1979 Gary Rowell achieved cult status amongst Sunderland fans by completing a hat trick at St James' Park in a 4-1 victory over Newcastle United.

1912 Record pre-WW1 attendance at Roker Park of 43,383 for the third round FA Cup tie against West Bromwich Albion.

FEBRUARY 25

2004 Two extra time goals by Tommy Smith secured a fifth round FA Cup replay victory at Birmingham City.

1985 Death of 1930s centre forward Harry Poulter aged 74. (see January 9th)

1961 Inside forward John Goodchild scored a first half hat trick in his only appearance during that season; a 4-2 victory at Leeds United. This turned out to be his final appearance for The Lads.

1950 A first half goal by Len Shackleton at Blackpool secured all of the points and moved Sunderland up into third position in the top flight.

FEBRUARY 26

2005 Cardiff City were beaten 2-1 on Wearside moving Sunderland into an automatic promotion spot; where they remained for the rest of the season.

1992 Sunderland won 3-2 at First Division West Ham United in a fifth round FA Cup replay thanks to a brace from John Byrne and a late winner from David Rush.

1983 A Gary Rowell penalty was the decisive strike as Sunderland beat Manchester City 3-2 at Roker Park in the 100th League meeting between the two sides.

1955 Charlie "Cannonball" Fleming netted a brace as Sunderland won 2-1 at Newcastle United in front of almost 63,000 fans.

25.02.2004 Tommy Smith

Vic Halom

FEBRUARY 27

1999 Sunderland drew 0-0 with Oxford United in the first ever pay per view televised game.

1982 Sunderland's home game against Notts County saw the final games of Barry Siddall, Alan Brown and John McGinley. Brown scored The Lads' only goal in a 1-1 draw.

1973 Vic Halom scored one of Sunderland's all time great goals in a 3-1 home fifth round FA Cup replay victory over First Division Manchester City.

1934 Birth of Stan Anderson in Horden; the first person to captain Sunderland, Newcastle United and Middlesbrough.

Stan Anderson

FEBRUARY 28

2001 Newly appointed England coach Sven Goran Eriksson gave Gavin McCann his debut, and only game, for England in a 3-0 friendly victory against Spain at Villa Park.

1987 A controversial last minute Mark Proctor penalty against Ipswich Town's stand-in keeper, defender Ian Cranson, gave The Lads a 1-0 victory.

1903 Sunderland won the Sheriff of London's Shield (forerunner to the Charity Shield) by beating Corinthians 3-0 at White Hart Lane.

1891 The Lads drew 3-3 with Notts County at Bramall Lane in their first FA Cup semi final. John Campbell had a late winner disallowed as the referee thought the ball had gone wide. Goal nets, not previously used, were thought to have been introduced as a result of the arguments following this decision.

FEBRUARY 29

1992 A first half John Byrne penalty gave The Lads all the points at home to Wolverhampton Wanderers.

1964 Second Division Sunderland drew 3-3 at top flight Manchester United in a sixth round FA Cup tie after leading 3-1 with only a few minutes to go. (see March 4th)

1936 Sunderland remained top of Division One even though they lost 3-2 at Preston North End; Patsy Gallacher and Bobby Gurney getting the Black Cats' goals.

1908 Right back Emerson Marples made his debut at Chelsea; the only Sunderland player to do so on this date.

29.02.1964 Johnny Crossan (10) scores a penalty at Old Trafford

MARCH 1

1999 Sunderland announced plans to increase the capacity of the Stadium of Light from 42,000 to 48,000, with the future possibility of extending it to 63,000. (see June 23rd and 28th)

1984 Manager Alan Durban sacked with Bryan 'Pop' Robson taking over as caretaker manager. (see March 5th)

1972 Only 8,273 spectators saw John Lathan's only hat trick for the Black Cats, in a Wednesday afternoon 3-2 home victory over Portsmouth. It was Roker Park's lowest League crowd for almost nineteen years.

1930 Birth of centre forward Ted Purdon in Johannesburg.

Alan Durban

MARCH 2

1974 Dennis Tueart and Bobby Kerr were sent off in a 2-0 home defeat by Middlesbrough.

1963 62,420 spectators witnessed a goal less draw at home to The Magpies that kept Sunderland second in Division Two. This is the highest attendance The Lads have played in front of for a League game outside of the top flight.

1922 Sunderland signed centre half Michael Gilhooley from Hull City for a British record fee of £5,250. Jock Paterson also joined from Leicester City for £3,790.

1870 Birth of Victorian era goal scorer Jimmy Millar in Annbank, Ayrshire; holder of a record four top flight Championship medals (shared with Teddy Doig).

MARCH 3

1996 Goals from Ball, Russell, Phil Gray and Bridges gave Sunderland a 4-0 away victory at Grimsby Town thus maintaining their automatic promotion spot.

1973 Jim Montgomery made his 459th first team appearance; at home to Oxford United, beating Len Ashurst's club record. (see October 6th)

1939 John Cochrane resigned as manager with Club Secretary George Crow stepping up into the position until Bill Murray was appointed. (see March 24th)

1922 Sunderland break the British transfer record again, only 24 hours after setting it, signing right back Warney Cresswell from South Shields for £5,500.

MARCH 4

1985 Sunderland beat Chelsea 3-2, 5-2 on aggregate, at Stamford Bridge in a highly charged Milk Cup semi final second leg. Colin West scored the third goal whilst policemen and a police horse chased a Chelsea fan across the pitch who had tried to attack former Blue Clive Walker.

1964 An estimated 70,000 spectators crammed into Roker Park to see a sixth round FA Cup replay against Manchester United with thousands more locked outside. The official attendance was only 46,727 as many people entered without paying when gates at the Roker End were lifted off their hinges. (see February 29th)

1961 Tottenham Hotspur's captain, Danny Blanchflower, reckoned the loudest noise he heard during his football career was when Willie McPheat scored the equaliser in a 1-1 sixth round FA Cup tie at Roker.

1950 A drawn Sunderland v Newcastle United game set Roker Park's record League attendance of 68,004.

MARCH 5

1994 Dariusz Kubicki became the first Pole to play for Sunderland when he made his debut against Notts County, two days after joining on loan from Aston Villa.

1984 Len Ashurst, the holder of Sunderland's record number of outfield appearances, was appointed manager with caretaker `Pop' Robson returning to his coaching role. (See March 1st)

1977 Sunderland scored six goals for the second successive home game; 6-0 win over West Ham United, and moved out of the top flight relegation zone for the first time for six months. (see February 22nd)

1938 Sunderland beat Spurs 1-0 thanks to a Raich Carter goal in a sixth round FA Cup tie in front of a record 75,038 people at White Hart Lane. This day also saw the death of Jackie Mordue at the age of 51.

MARCH 6

2006 Mick McCarthy was sacked as manager with assistant Academy Manager, and former captain, Kevin Ball taking temporary charge.

1976 Second Division Sunderland's FA Cup run was halted by a 1-0 home defeat by Third Division Crystal Palace in what turned out to be Northern Irish international Tom Finney's final game for The Lads.

1953 Birth of the youngest member of Sunderland's 1973 FA Cup winning team, Mick Horswill, in Annfield Plain.

1882 Irish international winger Harry Buckle born in Belfast. His grandson, Roy, managed a Sunderland themed pub in Charlie Hurley and Roy Keane's home town of Cork.

06.03.06 Caretaker boss Kevin Ball

MARCH 7

2004 Tommy Smith scored the only goal against Sheffield United to take Sunderland through to their twelfth FA Cup semi final.

1998 Niall Quinn scored the first hat trick by a Sunderland player at the Stadium of Light in a 4-1 victory over Stockport County.

1920 Birth of Willie Watson in Bolton-on-Dearne, Yorkshire; capped by England at both football and cricket. (see April 24th)

1891 Tom Porteous became the first Sunderland player to be capped by England; against Wales at his home, Newcastle Road, ground.

Tommy Smith

MARCH 8

1997 Second half goals from Michael Gray and John Mullin sealed a 2-1 home win in Manchester United's last game at Roker Park.

1996 Death of Alan Winston Brown aged 81. He was the first person to have two spells managing the Club; 1957-64 and 1968-72.

1958 South African centre forward Don "The Rhino" Kichenbrand scored on his debut at home to Sheffield Wednesday.

1933 Roker Park had its record attendance for the sixth round FA Cup replay against Derby County. Sunderland lost 1-0 in extra time on a Wednesday afternoon in front of 75,118 spectators.

MARCH 9

1999 Niall Quinn took over in goal for the final fifteen minutes at Bradford City when Thomas Sorensen had to leave the field injured. Quinn had netted what turned out to be the winning goal only four minutes earlier.

1992 A second half John Byrne goal earned Sunderland a replay at Stamford Bridge in a sixth round FA Cup tie.

1979 FA Cup winning captain Bobby Kerr moved to Blackpool on a free transfer.

1935 Second placed Sunderland played out a goalless draw with Division One leaders Arsenal in front of Highbury's record attendance; 73,295.

MARCH 10

2003 Howard Wilkinson and Steve Cotterill sacked as manager and assistant manager after only twenty seven games in charge.

1939 Birth of right back and former manager Len Ashurst in Liverpool.

1928 David Halliday scored his 100th League goal for Sunderland in his 103rd League game; v Huddersfield Town. (see January 19th)

1900 Birth of long serving player then manager Bill Murray in Aberdeen.

Len Ashurst

MARCH 11

2000 A second half Kevin Phillips penalty gave Sunderland a 1-1 draw at Anfield. This was the twenty fifth of his thirty goal haul that season. (see May 6th)

1974 Dennis Tueart and Mick Horswill transferred to Manchester City for £275,000 and £100,000 respectively with Tony Towers moving in the opposite direction for £125,000.

1972 Northern Irish international defender Martin Harvey suffered a knee injury against Norwich City which effectively ended his playing career after 358 appearances.

1964 Birth of left sided defender and midfielder Paul Hardyman in Portsmouth.

MARCH 12

2003 Ex-Eire manager Mick McCarthy appointed as Sunderland's third different manager that season.

1960 Allan O'Neill recorded his only hat trick for The Lads in a 4-0 home victory over Plymouth Argyle. He is the only player to score for Sunderland under two different surnames; Hope (1957) and his stepfather's surname O'Neill (1957-60).

1955 Two second half goals by Ted Purdon against Wolves sent Sunderland through to an FA Cup semi final meeting with Manchester City.

1910 English internationals Arthur Bridgett and George Holley scored a goal each and Harry Low a brace as The Lads comfortably beat Chelsea 4-1 at Stamford Bridge.

MARCH 13

2007 A last minute Daryl Murphy goal preserved Sunderland's unbeaten run as The Lads fought back to draw 2-2 with Stoke City at the Stadium of Light.

1998 Death of winger Tommy Reynolds aged 75 who had appeared in the seasons immediately after WW2.

1976 A brace from Bobby Kerr gave Sunderland a 2-0 win at Orient, which, despite their third place in Division Two, was their first away success for three months.

1920 Jackie Mordue's final game for Sunderland; a 2-0 home win over Middlesbrough, the club he signed for two months later.

Daryl Murphy

MARCH 14

1988 England U-15s beat their Brazilian counterparts 3-0 at Roker Park in front of 16,058 spectators. Future Sunderland players Lee Clark and Marcus Stewart scored two of the goals and Chris Makin came on as a substitute.

1963 Death of Robert Hogg aged 85; the first Sunderland player to score a hat trick against Newcastle United.
(see December 23rd)

1921 Charlie Buchan became the first Sunderland player to captain England when he led them to a goalless draw against Wales in Cardiff.

1896 Hugh Wilson became the first Sunderland player to be sent off in a first team game. He was dismissed for insulting referee Mr Kingscott in a 5-0 defeat at Stoke.

MARCH 15

2005 Sunderland's 5-1 defeat of Plymouth Argyle was unusual in that five different players got on the scoresheet; Whitehead, Arca, Stewart (penalty), Caldwell and Thornton.

1967 A fifth round FA Cup replay between Sunderland and Leeds United drew a record 57,892 crowd at Elland Road. The game ended 1-1 after extra time.
(see March 20th)

1928 Robert Kyle announced his decision to retire as Sunderland manager at the end of that season.

1909 George Holley scored on his England debut in a 2-0 win over Wales at the City Ground, Nottingham.

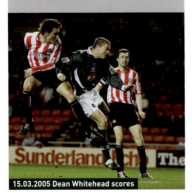
15.03.2005 Dean Whitehead scores

MARCH 16

1997 Substitutes Paul Stewart and Alex Rae scored for Sunderland in a 6-2 defeat at Chelsea; the first time more than one substitute had found the net for The Lads in the same game.

1985 In a dress rehearsal for the following week's Milk Cup final Sunderland defeated Norwich City 3-1 at Carrow Road. This was their first three goal haul in a League game away from home for almost two years.

1967 Half back Jim McNab transferred to Preston North End for £15,000 after almost eleven years on Wearside.

1908 Injured Sunderland keeper Dick Roose became the first player to be replaced by a substitute in an international match when Dai Davies, of Bolton, came on for him; Wales v England at Wrexham.

MARCH 17

2001 Sunderland twice recovered from a goal down to win 4-2 at Chelsea thanks to a brace from Don Hutchison and one each from Gavin McCann and Kevin Phillips.

1997 Former England international Chris Waddle signed from Bradford City for £75,000.

1996 Striker Phil Gray's final game for The Lads; a 2-0 away win at Birmingham City that put Sunderland top of Division One.

1973 Watson and Guthrie scored in the second half against Luton Town to set up an FA Cup semi final meeting with Arsenal at Hillsborough.

Chris Waddle

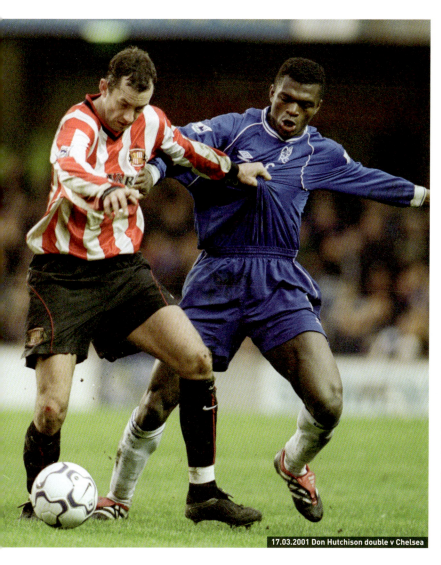

17.03.2001 Don Hutchison double v Chelsea

MARCH 18

1993 Sunderland born, and lifelong Black Cats fan, Mick Harford signed for £250,000 from Chelsea.

1992 A dramatic late Gordon Armstrong header at the Roker End clinched a 2-1 home win over Chelsea in a sixth round FA Cup replay.

1977 Record appearance holder Jim Montgomery moved to Birmingham City on a free transfer after completing a month long loan spell at St Andrews.

1869 Hugh Wilson, captain of "The Team of all the Talents" born in Mauchline, Ayrshire.

Mick Harford

MARCH 19

2005 A second half Chris Brown goal gave Sunderland all the points at home to Coventry City. This win put them top of The Championship where they remained for the rest of the season.

1994 Sunderland beat Watford 2-0 thanks to a brace from Craig Russell on what turned out to be David Rush's final appearance.

1949 Dickie Davis netted a hat trick at Deepdale, his first for Sunderland, in a 3-1 win against Preston North End.

1898 Ex-Sunderland player James Gillespie scored a hat trick for Scotland on his only international appearance; a 5-2 win against Wales at Motherwell.

MARCH 20

1967 George Herd and George Mulhall were sent off for disputing a last minute penalty for Leeds United in a fifth round FA Cup second replay at Boothferry Park, Hull. Johnny Giles converted the penalty giving Leeds a 2-1 victory.

1963 Nineteen year old Nick Sharkey scored five goals in a 7-1 win over Norwich City to equal Jimmy Millar's, Charlie Buchan's and Bobby Gurney's scoring record in a game. (see also February 2nd and December 7th)

1937 Charlie Thomson played his 147th consecutive first team game for Sunderland; a record that is unlikely to be beaten.

1925 Birth of player, coach and manger of Sunderland, Billy Elliott, in Bradford.

Nick Sharkey with the matchball from 1963.

MARCH 21

1970 Full back Len Ashurst played his 457th first team game thus equalling goalkeeper Ted Doig's appearance record. (see March 3rd and April 2nd)

1935 Birth of goal scoring legend Brian Clough in Middlesbrough.

1911 Forward Charlie Buchan was signed from Leyton for £1,200.

1903 Sunderland lost 1-0 at home to Sheffield Wednesday. The crowd were incensed by the referee's performance and stoned his brake as it left the ground. As punishment the Football League closed Roker Park for the last League game of the season. (see April 18th)

A statue of Brian Clough by sculptor Vivien Matlock was unveiled in his home town of Middlesbrough in 2007.

MARCH 22

1995 Brett Angell and Dominic Matteo signed on the eve of the transfer deadline from Everton for £600,000 and on loan from Liverpool respectively. (see March 31st)

1986 Cameron Duncan saved a penalty at Grimsby Town in a 1-1 draw on his Sunderland debut.

1952 Outside right Len Duns played his final game for Sunderland; a goalless home draw with Preston North End, after 18 years at the Club.

1909 Sunderland lost 8-1 at Blackburn Rovers in what turned out to be right back John Johnston's only game for The Lads.

Brett Angell

MARCH 23

2000 Diminutive Honduran international striker, Milton Nunez, signed from PAOK Salonika, Greece, for £1.6 million.

1976 Sunderland dropped only their second home point of the season with a 1-1 draw against Bristol City. Their only other dropped point during this promotion winning season of 19 home wins came against Bristol Rovers. (see November 22nd)

1968 Malcolm Moore, on his debut, became the first substitute to score for Sunderland at Roker Park; in a 1-1 draw against Coventry City.

1912 Scottish forward James Gemmell's final game for Sunderland; a 1-0 home victory over Woolwich Arsenal. Half back, turned emergency centre forward, Harry Low got the only goal, his sixth in seven appearances in this position.

MARCH 24

1990 A scintillating performance from Kieron Brady ensured a 4-3 home victory over West Ham United. The eighteen year old scored with an overhead kick, won a penalty and provided the cross for Gary Owers' decisive goal.

1985 Sunderland's first League Cup final ended in a 1-0 defeat against Norwich City. The only goal, the 100th Sunderland had conceded in this competition since its start in 1960, was an own goal by Gordon Chisholm. Clive Walker missed an opportunity to equalise when his second half penalty struck the outside of the post.

1939 Ex-player Bill Murray appointed as manager with caretaker manager George Crow returning to his role as Club Secretary. (see March 3rd)

1934 Bobby Gurney scored a hat trick at West Bromwich Albion but still ended up on the losing side as Sunderland went down 6-5 at The Hawthorns.

MARCH 25

2000 Sunderland beat Everton 2-1 thanks to goals from Summerbee and Phillips. It was their first win of the new century and ended a run of eleven games without a victory which had seen them drop from 3rd to 8th in the Premiership.

1989 Marco Gabbiadini was sent off for retaliating with an Ipswich Town defender after successfully converting a penalty to complete his hat trick in a 4-0 home win. This game featured the only appearance for The Lads of Alan Hay, limited to 28 minutes due to a calf strain.

1974 Death of former centre half Alex Lockie aged 78.

1907 Scottish international left back James Watson's final game for Sunderland; at Manchester United, after seven years service on Wearside.

MARCH 26

1997 Scottish international winger Allan Johnston signed from Rennes, France, for £500,000.

1927 John "Paddy" Bell had an eventful debut at home to Leeds United. He saved a first half penalty then was stretchered off after fifty minutes having been kicked in the stomach. Sunderland won 6-2 with Halliday and Ramsay bagging hat tricks.

1900 Sunderland played in front of their lowest League crowd; a Monday afternoon re-arranged game at Stoke played after three hours of heavy snow fall. Contemporary press reports state the attendance ranging from a few hundred to no more than a thousand.

1892 The "Team of all The Talents" beat Aston Villa 2-1 to go top of the First Division for the first time in their history.

MARCH 27

2004 Sunderland beat Derby County 2-1 at home thanks to goals from John Oster and Tommy Smith. This was Colin Cooper's third and final appearance for The Lads in a career that totalled only twenty minutes.

1979 Debut of former England right back Steve Whitworth in 1-0 away victory at promotion rivals Stoke City.

1965 Death of Francis Cuggy aged 75. He formed part of the famous "Sunderland Triangle" with Charlie Buchan and Jackie Mordue either side of WW1.

1862 Birth of John Grayston in Halifax, inaugural secretary for Sunderland & District Teachers' Association Football Club.

MARCH 28

1998 Sunderland maintained their automatic promotion place with a 2-1 home victory over Bury; Lee Clark and Kevin Phillips (penalty) scored for The Lads.

1985 Striker Colin West transferred to Watford for £100,000.

1952 Death of pre-WW1 right back Andrew McCombie aged 75.

1935 Raich Carter and Bert Davis sent off in a 6-0 defeat at Ayresome Park. This was the first occasion in which two Sunderland players had been dismissed in the same game.

Colin West

MARCH 29

1995 Mick Buxton sacked as manager and replaced by Peter Reid on a temporary basis until the end of the season. (see May 22nd)

1993 Death of post WW2 right back Jack Stelling aged 68. (see December 20th)

1986 Tony Ford became the first loan player to score on his debut when he netted after coming on as a substitute for Paul Lemon against Bradford City.

1913 Sunderland drew 0-0 with Burnley at Bramall Lane in an FA Cup semi final; the last time they have drawn a semi final. (see April 2nd)

Mick Buxton

MARCH 30

1996 Substitute Michael Bridges scored two late goals to seal a 3-2 home victory over Huddersfield Town to keep Sunderland top of Division One. This was the team's ninth successive win and put Bridges in the record book as Sunderland's youngest player to score a brace at 17 years 238 days.

1959 Sunderland suffered their worst League defeat outside of the top flight; 6-0 at Orient.

1955 Newcastle United and York City met in the only FA Cup semi final to be staged at Roker Park. This replay was also the first all ticket game at the stadium.

1912 England winger Arthur Bridgett's final game for Sunderland; against Manchester City. He is the only Sunderland player to have scored over 100 goals without achieving a hat trick.

MARCH 31

2007 A second half free kick from substitute Ross Wallace gave Sunderland all of the points at promotion rivals Cardiff City.

1995 Sunderland fined £2,500 for fielding an ineligible player, Dominic Matteo, against Barnsley on 24th March. Although signed on transfer deadline day not all of the relevant paperwork had been received in time by The Football League. As a result Matteo's loan spell was immediately terminated and he headed back to Liverpool.

1969 Burnley v Sunderland game abandoned at half time due to a waterlogged pitch with The Lads losing 1-0.

1962 Brian Clough scored the only goal on his first visit back to Ayresome Park in what was to be Peter Wakeham's final appearance for the Black Cats.

APRIL

APRIL 1

2006 Striker Jon Stead scored his first goal for Sunderland in his 30th game; at Goodison Park, Everton. He had waited just over 1700 playing minutes for it.

1995 A late Craig Russell strike gave manager Peter Reid victory over Sheffield United in his first game in charge.

1911 Debut of future Sunderland captain and record League goalscorer, Charlie Buchan, at White Hart Lane in a 1-1 draw.

1893 Sunderland lost 2-1 at Bolton Wanderers however still clinched their second successive League Championship as nearest rivals Preston lost at Newton Heath.

Jon Stead

APRIL 2

2003 England beat Turkey 2-0 in a Euro 2004 qualifying game at the Stadium of Light.

1988 A first half Marco Gabbiadini goal gives Sunderland maximum points at Grimsby Town to regain top spot in Division Three.

1913 Sunderland beat Burnley 3-2 at St Andrews in an FA Cup semi final replay to keep the dream of a League and Cup double alive. (see March 29th)

1904 Scottish goalkeeper Ted Doig played his 457th and final game for Sunderland; against Manchester City. This record has only been surpassed by Len Ashurst and Jim Montgomery. (see March 21st and March 3rd respectively)

Ted Doig

APRIL 3

1982 Loek Ursem became the first Dutch player to appear for The Lads when he came on as a substitute against Middlesbrough. This was also Kevin Arnott's final game.

1974 Centre half Dave Watson became the first Sunderland player to represent England for almost twelve years when he made his debut in a goalless draw against Portugal in Lisbon. He was partnered in central defence by former Black Cat Colin Todd.

1926 Bobby Gurney scored on his Sunderland debut in a 3-2 defeat at West Ham United.

1886 First game at the Newcastle Road ground; a friendly against Darlington that ended in a 3-1 victory with Jimmy Hunter scoring Sunderland's first goal at their new ground.

APRIL 4

2004 Sunderland lost 1-0 at Old Trafford to Millwall in an all Division One FA Cup semi final.

1989 Brian Atkinson and Paul Williams made their debuts in a 2-1 victory over Plymouth Argyle in front only 8,001 spectators; Roker Park's lowest League gate for 36 years.

1936 Debut of Sunderland's first FA Cup winning goalkeeper John Mapson in a 5-0 victory over Portsmouth.

1929 Birth of Jimmy Adamson in Ashington; Sunderland manager between 1976 and 1978.

04.04.04 Semi-final heartbreak.

APRIL 5

2005 An early Marcus Stewart goal was enough to give Championship leaders Sunderland victory at second placed Wigan Athletic.

1992 John Byrne kept up his record of scoring in every round of the FA Cup with the only goal against Norwich City in the semi final at Hillsborough.

1901 The scheduled Good Friday derby against Newcastle United at St James' Park was postponed without a ball being kicked. An estimated 70,000 people were inside the ground and could not be cleared off the pitch to allow the game to start.

1890 Sunderland beat Aston Villa 7-2 in a friendly at Newcastle Road which led to them being dubbed "The Team of all The Talents".

APRIL 6

2004 Welsh international midfielder Carl Robinson made his debut in a 2-1 victory over Wimbledon in Sunderland's first ever visit to The Dons' new home in Milton Keynes.

1994 Don Goodman became the first Sunderland substitute to be sent off when he saw red at Millwall.

1935 Patsy Gallacher became the first Sunderland player to be sent off twice in the same season when he was dismissed at The Hawthorns; he had earlier been sent off on September 22nd at home to Derby County.

1885 Birth of England international Arthur Brown in Gainsborough. He was the only one of the five forwards not to score in the 9-1 record away victory over Newcastle United. (see June 20th and December 5th)

John Byrne

APRIL 7

2007 The Lads beat former manager Mick McCarthy's Wolves 2-1 to maintain their promotion surge courtesy of goals from Daryl Murphy and Ross Wallace.

1973 Sunderland beat First Division Arsenal 2-1 in an FA Cup semi final at Hillsborough thanks to a goal in each half by Vic Halom and Billy Hughes.

1940 Death of Sunderland's first top flight championship winning captain Hugh Wilson aged 71.

1928 David Halliday netted his 30th League goal of the season in only his 33rd League appearance; a 2-1 away victory at Bolton Wanderers.

07/04/1973 - FA Cup semi-final vs Arsenal

APRIL 8

2006 Sunderland v Fulham game abandoned after 21 minutes due to snow and surface water with The Lads losing 1-0. (see May 4th)

1980 Sunderland hit top spot in Division Two for the first time in the season thanks to a first half 'Pop' Robson strike and a Stan Cummins free kick giving them a 2-1 victory at Shrewsbury Town.

1942 Birth of Sunderland's youngest defender, full back Cec Irwin, in Ellington, Northumberland. (see September 20th)

1922 Ex-Sunderland player Barney Travers was banned from football for life for trying to fix the result of the South Shields v Fulham match on March 18th 1922 by offering South Shields £20 to lose.

APRIL 9

2005 Brian Deane became Sunderland's oldest debutant, aged 37 years 58 days, when he appeared as the third substitute at home to Reading.

1992 Former Sunderland striker Vic Halom unsuccessfully stood as Liberal Democrat candidate for Sunderland North in a Parliamentary General Election.

1892 Sunderland lost 1-0 at Notts County to end their record run of thirteen consecutive League victories.

1859 Birth of Tom Watson, Sunderland's first manager (1889 – 1896), in Heaton, Newcastle.

APRIL 10

1999 Goals from Niall Quinn and Allan Johnston sealed a 2-0 home victory over Huddersfield Town.

1976 A 3-0 home victory over Blackburn Rovers took Sunderland to the top of Division Two with only four games of the season left.

1965 Birth of Thomas Hauser, Sunderland's first German player, in Schopfheim. (see April 13th)

1957 Sunderland fined £5,000 and directors punished for their part in illegally paying players. Bill Ditchburn and Bill Martin were permanently banned from football.
(see also January 7th, April 25th and May 17th)

Allan Johnston

APRIL 11

1977 First half goals from Kevin Arnott and Tony Towers (penalty) gave Sunderland a 2-1 win over Manchester United which moved them out of the relegation zone.

1952 Sunderland's best win for just over 17 years saw them demolish Huddersfield Town 7-1 at Roker Park.

1934 Roker Park had its lowest accurately recorded attendance for a first team game; 3,841 turned up to see an end of season Wednesday afternoon game against Manchester City.
(see December 12th)

1896 The "Team of all The Talents" finished outside of the top two in Division One for the first time since their inaugural season following a 1-0 away win at Small Heath. This was their sixth win in the last seven games.

APRIL 12

2003 Sunderland lost 2-0 at Birmingham City to confirm their inevitable relegation from the Premiership with five games of the season still remaining. The game also marked goalkeeper Mart Poom's debut.

1999 Four goals from Kevin Phillips at Gigg Lane helped seal a promotion guaranteeing 5-2 victory over Bury in front of Sky TV's cameras.

1963 Roker Park had its last crowd of over sixty thousand when 62,138 attended on Good Friday to see what turned out to be Stan Matthews' final game on Wearside. The game against Stoke City ended 0-0.

1913 Charlie Buchan followed up his nap hand against Liverpool earlier in the season with a hat trick at Anfield as Sunderland won 5-2 to complete a high scoring double over Liverpool (see December 7th).

APRIL 13

2002 The Stadium of Light attracted a record attendance, 48,355, for the visit of Liverpool. The game, which ended 1-0 to Liverpool, also saw the dismissal of Claudio Reyna.

1991 Thomas Hauser became the first German to score in the top flight of English football when he netted at Southampton in a 3-1 defeat.

1981 Ken Knighton sacked as Sunderland manager, a job he had held for less than two years, with Mick Docherty taking over in a caretaker capacity.

1936 Sunderland won 7-2, their third win by this score that season, at Birmingham to claim their sixth, and so far last, top flight championship.

APRIL 14

2006 A goalless draw at Old Trafford, in front of 72,519, finally marked the long expected relegation from the Premiership.

2001 Death of former Scottish international, and cousin of George Kinnell, Jim Baxter aged 61.

1992 Sunderland played their fourth of ten games in April of this year due to fixture congestion caused by their FA Cup run. This Tuesday night game in wet conditions ended with a 3-0 victory over Ipswich Town.

1922 Jock Paterson netted a hat trick in his eighth game for the Club; a 6-2 home victory over Bolton Wanderers.

APRIL 15

1995 Gary Bennett made his final Sunderland appearance in a 1-1 draw at home to Luton Town.

1970 The Lads one goal defeat at home to Liverpool confirmed relegation back to Division Two for the second time in their history.

1959 Len Shackleton's testimonial game at Roker Park against an All Stars XI attracted 26,176 with Shack's team winning 5-4.

1893 Sunderland became the first League club to score one hundred goals in a season (only 30 games) when they netted their third goal in a 3-2 last day victory at Burnley.

Gary Bennett

APRIL 16

1999 A 3-1 Friday night victory at Barnsley sealed the Division One title for already promoted Sunderland. (see April 12th and May 9th)

1987 Manager Lawrie McMenemy left Sunderland and was replaced by caretaker manager Bob Stokoe.

1983 Goalkeeper Chris Turner sustained a fractured skull in a League game at Norwich City; Nick Pickering took over between the sticks.

1892 Sunderland's 6-1 home victory over Blackburn Rovers clinched their first League Championship with two games of the season still remaining. It also meant that they had won all 15 home games played that season (13 League and 2 FA Cup).

APRIL 17

2005 Michael Ingham and Sean Thornton made their final appearances for The Lads in a 2-2 draw at Portman Road that kept Sunderland's promotion challenge alive.

1972 Left back Joe Bolton made his debut as a 17 year old in a 5-0 home victory over Watford; their best win for just over 8 years.

1909 Former England forward and Sunderland coach Billy Hogg's final game for the Black Cats ended in a 4-2 away victory at Bristol City.

1897 Sunderland played the first of four Test Matches, at Notts County, to determine whether they remained in the top flight having finished the season next to bottom.

Billy Hogg

APRIL 18

1981 Striker Tom Ritchie scored a hat trick in a 3-0 home victory over Birmingham City after failing to find the net in his first eleven games since signing from Bristol City.

1964 Goals by George Herd and John Crossan gave Sunderland a 2-1 victory over Charlton Athletic that sealed their first ever promotion to Division One.

1936 Top flight champions Sunderland reached 109 League goals, their highest in any season, with a 4-3 home win over Huddersfield Town.

1903 Sunderland played their first home League game against Middlesbrough at St James' Park because Roker Park had been closed as punishment for crowd disturbances. (see March 21st)

APRIL 19

1997 Teesside born Darren Williams scored the only goal in a relegation battle against Middlesbrough at The Riverside Stadium.

1976 A 2-1 Easter Monday home victory over Bolton Wanderers, in front of Roker Park's last crowd in excess of 50,000, saw The Lads promoted back to the top flight.

1930 Bobby Gurney scored four goals in a 6-0 away victory at Liverpool.

1913 Sunderland lost their first ever FA Cup final 1-0 against Aston Villa in front of a record crowd of 120,081 at Crystal Palace.

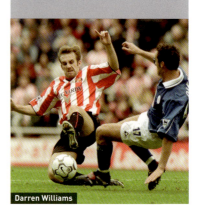

Darren Williams

APRIL 20

1996 Sunderland clinched promotion to the Premiership without playing as their nearest rivals, Derby County, failed to beat Birmingham City.

1989 Death of former winger Len Duns aged 72 who served Sunderland for almost nineteen years either side of WW2.

1968 Centre half Charlie Hurley scored his 26th, and final, goal for Sunderland when he opened the scoring in a 2-0 home win over Arsenal.

1895 A 2-1 victory at home to second placed Everton enabled Sunderland to claim their third League Championship in four years.

APRIL 21

2007 Sunderland's best unbeaten League start to a calendar year (14 wins & 3 draws) was halted at Layer Road, Colchester, by a 3-1 defeat.

2004 Mart Poom became the first Sunderland keeper to be sent off when he was shown a red card for conceding a first half penalty at Crystal Palace.

1994 Death of Sunderland goal scoring legend Bobby Gurney aged 86.

1949 Sunderland won 2-1 against Manchester United to end a record run of six consecutive draws.

21.04.2004 Mart Poom sent off

APRIL 22

2006 Julio Arca's final appearance for The Lads was at Fratton Park, Portsmouth, in a 2-1 defeat. This meant that Sunderland had not won a game that kicked off at 3 pm on a Saturday during that season.

2000 A brace from Kevin Phillips, his 28th and 29th goals of the season, gave Sunderland all of the points at relegation threatened Sheffield Wednesday.

1935 Thomas Urwin became Sunderland's oldest player, 39 years 76 days, when he made his final appearance, at Preston North End. He was the assistant trainer and it was his first game for over three years.

1925 Death of the first Sunderland player to score an FA Cup hat trick, John Breconridge, aged 59. (see October 27th)

APRIL 23

2005 A second half Steve Caldwell header at the Stadium of Light gave Sunderland a promotion winning 2-1 victory over Leicester City.

1963 The League Cup semi final second leg against Aston Villa was finally played more that three months after the first leg. The goalless draw at Villa Park meant Sunderland lost 3-1 on aggregate. (see January 12th)

1898 James Chalmers scored the final goal at Newcastle Road in a 4-0 victory over Nottingham Forest.

1892 Sunderland won 7-1 at Darwen after beating them 7-0 at home earlier in the season thus recording their highest aggregate score against a team in one season. (see December 12th)

Steve Caldwell

Gordon Armstrong

APRIL 24

2004 Death of former international footballer and cricketer Willie Watson aged 84. (see March 7th)

1985 Gordon Armstrong made the first of over 400 first team appearances for Sunderland when he played at West Bromwich Albion.

1967 Birth of French keeper Lionel Perez in Bagnols-sur-Ceze.

1915 Charlie Buchan scored Sunderland's last League goal before football was halted due to WW1, in a 5-0 end of season home victory over Tottenham Hotspur. (see August 30th)

Lionel Perez

APRIL 25

1998 Sunderland maintained their chance of automatic promotion with a 3-0 home victory over Stoke City; the second goal being Kevin Phillips' 30th goal of the season.

1979 A 6-2 victory over Sheffield United, that included a Wilf Rostron hat trick, was sufficient to put Sunderland top of Division Two on goal difference.

1957 Fourteen Sunderland players were suspended "sine die" by The Football League for receiving illegal payments. (see also January 7th, April 10th and May 17th)

1903 Football League observers attended the Newcastle v Sunderland game to check that The Magpies did not deliberately lose the game thus handing Sunderland the League Championship. The Lads lost 1-0 and Sheffield Wednesday took the title.

APRIL 26

2008 An injury time goal from substitute Daryl Murphy sealed a 3-2 home win over Middlesbrough and guaranteed that Sunderland remained in the Premier League.

1958 Relegation was tasted for the first time as Sunderland's 68 year continuous tenure of Division One ended despite a 2-0 victory at Fratton Park, Portsmouth.

1913 A 3-1 victory at Bolton Wanderers sealed Sunderland's fifth League Championship.

1897 Sunderland beat Newton Heath 2-0, thanks to a brace from James Gillespie, in the end of season Test Match series to preserve their top flight status. (see April 17th)

26.04.2008

APRIL 27

2007 A 25 yard Carlos Edwards drive sealed a 3-2 home victory over Burnley in front of Sky TV cameras to virtually seal Sunderland's immediate return to the Premiership.

1996 Sunderland lifted the Division One Championship trophy after a goalless draw with West Bromwich Albion.

1961 Birth of Sunderland's youngest captain, Rob Hindmarch, in Stannington, Northumberland.

1929 Centre forward David Halliday scored his 11th hat trick for Sunderland as they beat West Ham United 4-1. This broke the record, set by Jimmy Millar, of ten hat tricks. It also took his goals tally to a seasonal record of 43. (see September 7th)

APRIL 28

2001 Scottish centre forward Kevin Kyle made his debut as a substitute for Niall Quinn in a 1-0 away victory at Southampton.

1999 Caretaker England boss Kevin Keegan gave debuts to Kevin Phillips and Michael Gray in the 1-1 friendly against Hungary. This was the first time two Sunderland players had appeared in the same England side since 1926.

1984 Sunderland won a bruising relegation battle at Roker Park against Birmingham City courtesy of two Leighton James penalties. Both sides had a player dismissed; Hindmarch for The Lads and Wearside born Mick Harford for The Blues.

1965 Goals from Ashurst, Mulhall and Hood sealed a 3-0 victory over Sheffield Wednesday in George Hardwick's last game as Sunderland manager.

39

APRIL 29

2007 Sunderland's first immediate return to the top flight following relegation was confirmed when nearest rivals Derby County lost at Crystal Palace. This was a triumph not only for the players but for the new manager and chairman partnership of Roy Keane and Niall Quinn.

1978 Left back Joe Bolton scored two first half goals at home to Charlton Athletic then put a second half penalty over the bar thus denying him from becoming the first Sunderland defender to score a hat trick.

1925 Legendary goal scorer David Halliday signed from Dundee for £4,000.

1899 Birth of Sunderland's most prolific penalty scorer, Billy Clunas, in Johnstone, Renfrewshire.

APRIL 30

1994 Sunderland beat Tranmere Rovers at Roker Park 3-2, after being two goals up within the first three minutes, courtesy of a brace from Phil Gray and a Craig Russell strike.

1988 An Eric Gates goal at Port Vale gave Sunderland victory and immediate promotion back to Division Two.

1973 Trevor Swinburne made his debut, and Ian Porterfield and Dennis Tueart were rested, in the 1-1 League draw at Orient on the Monday night before the FA Cup final. This was the Black Cats' 8th game in twenty days as the FA Cup run fixture backlog took its toll.

1913 Champions Sunderland set a new top flight points record with a final day 1-0 home win over Bradford City thanks to Charlie Buchan's 30th goal of the season. This was in spite of failing to win any of the first seven games of the season.

MAY

MAY 1

1993 Sunderland saved their best performance of the season for their last home game. The Black Cats beat third placed Portsmouth 4-1 with Don Goodman converting two penalties and Pompey having two players red carded.

1970 Roker Park staged its first competitive European game, in front of only 3,764 spectators, when Lazio were the opponents in an Anglo-Italian Cup tie.

1937 Preston North End were defeated 3-1 in the FA Cup final, thanks to goals from Gurney, Carter and Burbanks, enabling Hendon born Raich Carter to become the first Sunderland captain to lift this famous trophy. It was the first time the final had been shown live on television, albeit only the second half.

1920 Sunderland's final League match of the season, at home to Liverpool, was declared a benefit game to celebrate Bob Kyle's fifteen years as manager.

Don Goodman

Raich Carter receives the FA Cup in 1937

MAY 2

1988 A 3-1 home triumph over Northampton Town gave Sunderland the Third Division title in front of almost thirty thousand people.

1981 A first half Stan Cummins goal at Anfield ensured that Sunderland were not relegated after only one season back in Division One. This game marked the final appearances of Sam Allardyce and Joe Bolton.

1925 Record League goalscorer Charlie Buchan made his final appearance in red and white stripes in a 1-1 draw at home to Burnley.

1890 Sunderland, represented by Rev. Robinson. Hindle and James Marr, successfully made their case for inclusion into the Football League at a meeting in the Douglas Hotel, Manchester.
(see September 13th)

Sam Allardyce

MAY 3

1998 As a result of other games a 2-1 away win at Swindon Town was not good enough to give Sunderland automatic promotion to the Premiership. Their 90 points from 46 games set a record for a side finishing third in Division One.

1997 Sunderland played their last ever League game at Roker Park. Allan Johnston got the final goal in a 3-0 victory over Everton.

1969 Sunderland beat West Bromwich Albion 6-0 in the FA Youth Cup final second leg at Roker Park to capture the trophy 6-3 on aggregate.

1922 Birth of "The Clown Prince of Soccer" Len Shackleton in Bradford.

MAY 4

2006 Sunderland recorded their first home win of the season, at their final attempt; a 2-1 victory over Fulham in a re-arranged game. (see April 8th)

2004 A first half header from Carl Robinson against Norwich City ensured Sunderland's place in the promotion play offs and, as a result of other games, sealed The Canaries' promotion to the Premiership as champions.

1969 Charlie Hurley made the last of his record 38 international appearances as a Sunderland player in Eire's 2-1 World Cup qualifier home defeat to Czechoslovakia.

1943 Birth of Scottish forward Dominic Sharkey in Helensburgh.

MAY 5

2001 Goals from Kilbane, Quinn and Phillips (the last time the latter pair scored in the same game) gave Sunderland a 3-2 home victory over Charlton Athletic.

1973 Ian Porterfield's goal against Leeds United meant Sunderland were the first Second Division side to lift the FA Cup since 1931.

1928 The Black Cats beat Middlesbrough 3-0 at Ayresome Park in Bob Kyle's last match in charge to avoid relegation from the top flight.

1888 Sunderland players Monaghan, Oliver and Richardson played in newly formed Sunderland Albion's first ever game; against Shankhouse Black Watch.

05.05.1973

MAY 6

2007 Sunderland were crowned champions of The Championship after a 5-0 demolition of Luton Town at Kenilworth Road.

2000 Kevin Phillips scored his 30th League goal of the season, at home to West Ham United, becoming the first Sunderland player since Raich Carter and Bobby Gurney, in 1936, to achieve this feat in the top flight.

1950 The final home game of the season against Chelsea saw Sunderland finish third, their highest post WW2 finish, and ensured that the aggregate home League attendance topped one million for the only time in the Club's history.

1915 Death of manager of "The Team of all the Talents" Tom Watson in Liverpool aged 56.

06.05.2007

MAY 7

2006 Gary Breen, Justin Hoyte, Anthony Le Tallec and Andy Welsh all played their last game for Sunderland in the final Premiership game of the season at Aston Villa.

1995 Tony Norman made his final appearance for The Lads and Martin Smith scored for the third consecutive game in a 2-2 home draw with West Bromwich Albion.

1988 Keith Bertschin scored Sunderland's last goal in Division Three in a 4-1 win at Rotherham United. (see August 15th)

1923 Goalkeeper Albert McInroy was signed in a toilet of Manchester's Grand Hotel two minutes after his contract expired with Leyland Motors.

MAY 8

2005 A near capacity Stadium of Light crowd saw a Carl Robinson goal give Sunderland a win over Stoke City. The game ended with the presentation of the Championship trophy to captain Gary Breen.

1993 Sunderland were easily beaten 3-1 at Notts County but avoided relegation to the third tier thanks to other clubs around them losing.

1955 Sunderland started a post season American tour with a 7-2 victory over an American League Stars team at Ebbets Field, Brooklyn. (see June 5th)

1936 Birth of Scottish international outside left George Mulhall in Standburn, near Falkirk.

08.05.1993

08.05.2005

MAY 9

1999 The final game of the season saw the Black Cats record their 31st victory, at home to Birmingham City, setting a new Division One points record of 105. The 31 wins and only 3 defeats were also divisional records.

1992 Sunderland became the lowest placed FA Cup finalist (they had finished 18th in Division Two) since Leicester City in 1949 when they played, and lost 2-0, against Liverpool.

1987 A 3-2 home defeat by Barnsley meant Sunderland had to take part in the end of season play offs to determine whether they stayed in Division Two or were relegated. (see May 17th)

1973 A crowd of 43,265 were in party mood to greet the FA Cup winners for the final home game against Queens Park Rangers. However the mood changed as first the trophy, on display in front of the dug out, was knocked over by a QPR clearance, Horswill was sent off for retaliation followed by a pitch invasion and finally two late Stan Bowles goals gave Rangers a 3-0 victory.

MAY 10

1998 Richard Ord made his final appearance for The Lads, as substitute for Chris Makin, in a first leg play off at Sheffield United.

1947 Jack Jones played his last game for Sunderland, a 2-1 away win at Grimsby Town, before joining the club's training staff for the next 21 years.

1923 Charlie Buchan scored and Warney Cresswell appeared at right back in England's 4-1 win over France in Paris.

1907 Centre forward Sam Raybould signed from Liverpool.

Richard Ord

MAY 11

2003 Freddy Ljungberg became the first opposition player to score a hat trick at the Stadium of Light as Arsenal beat Sunderland 4-0. This game marked the final appearances of Jody Craddock, Gavin McCann, Kevin Phillips, Richie Ryan and Thomas Sorensen.

1997 Sunderland lost to a late Wimbledon goal and were relegated from the Premiership with a record points total (40).

1991 Goals from Marco Gabbiadini and Gary Bennett were not enough as Sunderland lost 3-2 at Maine Road, in front of 15,000 travelling fans, and were relegated after only one year in the top flight.

1968 Sunderland's last win at Old Trafford prevented Manchester United from retaining the League title. Suggett and Mulhall netted in the 2-1 victory only eighteen days before United beat Benfica to lift the European Cup.

MAY 12

1984 Bryan `Pop' Robson became Sunderland's oldest goal scorer, aged 38 years 183 days, when he got the second in a 2-0 victory at Leicester City; his final appearance after three spells with the Club.

1980 Sunderland beat FA Cup winners West Ham United 2-0 in front of a full house of over 47,000 fans to clinch promotion to Division One. Kevin Arnott and Stan Cummins got the decisive goals either side of half time.

1951 Billy Bingham made his international debut for Northern Ireland against France in Belfast.

1899 Scottish international Hugh Wilson transferred to Bedminster, of the Southern League, after nine years with the Club.

John Mullin

MAY 13

1998 Two first half goals in misty conditions sealed a play off semi final 3-2 aggregate victory over Sheffield United. In one of the match reports the Stadium of Light was referred to as the Stadium of Sound due to the passion of the home fans.

1997 John Mullin scored the last ever goal at Roker Park as Sunderland beat Liverpool 1-0 in a post season friendly to mark the end of football at the ground after 99 years.

1990 A last minute Paul Hardyman penalty was saved by Newcastle keeper John Burridge leaving the play off first leg goalless. However Hardyman was sent off for his follow up challenge as the ball broke loose so missed the return leg at St James' Park. (see May 16th)

1964 Republic of Ireland captain Charlie Hurley scored both of his international goals in a 4-1 win against Norway in Oslo. He played at centre forward instead of centre half in this friendly.

MAY 14

2004 A Marcus Stewart penalty and a goal from Kevin Kyle meant Sunderland came away from Selhurst Park with a 3-2 deficit after the first leg of the play offs. (see May 17th)

2002 Niall Quinn's benefit game at the Stadium of Light between Sunderland and Eire raised £1 million for charity.

1987 Sunderland lost the first of the Division Two relegation play offs 3-2 at Gillingham with Mark Proctor getting both of the goals. (see May 17th)

1983 Internationals Ally McCoist and Frank Worthington made their final appearances in red and white stripes in a 1-1 home draw against West Bromwich Albion.

14.05.2004 Marcus Stewart

MAY 15

1984 Midfielder Paul Bracewell ended his first of three spells on Wearside by joining Everton for £275,000.

1982 Manchester City were the visitors for the final home game of the season. A first half Mick Buckley strike sealed the points for the Black Cats leaving them one place above the top flight relegation zone.

1975 Centre forward Mel Holden signed from Preston North End for £120,000.

1909 Sunderland started their first post season European tour with a 3-2 win over Torna Club of Budapest. (see June 1st)

Paul Bracewell

MAY 16

1990 Goals from Eric Gates and Marco Gabbiadini sealed a 2-0 win at St James' Park in the play off second leg sending Sunderland through to a Wembley play off final against Swindon Town.

1943 Overnight German air raids left a bomb crater in Roker Park's pitch and destroyed the club house in the corner of the Roker End.

1942 Cliff Whitelum scored the winner against Grimsby Town to seal a 3-2 semi final victory and confirm Sunderland's place in the War League Cup final. (see May 23rd)

1908 Charles Bellany Thomson, captain of the 1913 League Championship and FA Cup runners up team, signed from Heart of Midlothian for £350.

MAY 17

2004 Crystal Palace beat Sunderland 5-4 on penalties at the Stadium of Light after the two legged Division One play off ended 4-4 on aggregate. This was the final appearance of Phil Babb, Joachim Bjorklund, Jason McAteer and Tommy Smith. (see May 14th)

1987 Sunderland won 4-3 on the day against Gillingham but lost on away goals following a 6-6 aggregate score in the Division Two relegation play offs. As a result the Black Cats dropped to the Third Division for the first time in their history. (see May 14th)

1970 John Tones, making his debut as a substitute, scored Sunderland's first competitive goal on foreign soil; against Lazio in an Anglo-Italian Cup tie.

1957 The suspensions were lifted on fourteen Sunderland players found guilty of receiving illegal payments. (see also January 7th, April 10th and April 25th)

17.05.2004 Jason McAteer's penalty saved by Nico Claesen

MAY 18

2001 Expensive misfit Nicolas Medina signed from Argentinos Juniors for £3.5 million.

1963 A Tommy Harmer goal for Chelsea beat Sunderland 1-0 at Roker Park. Chelsea subsequently won their final game 7-0 to deny Sunderland promotion to Division One on goal average.

1930 Outside left Jimmy Connor made his debut for Scotland in a 2-0 win over France in Paris.

1890 Sunderland's first League Championship winning captain, Hugh Wilson, signed from Newmilns, Scotland, for £70.

Nicolas Medina

MAY 19

1977 Sunderland lost 2-0 at Everton and were relegated to Division Two because the two nearest rivals, Coventry City and Bristol City, played out a 2-2 draw to gain the point each of them needed to stay up.

1970 England and Germany Schoolboys played out a goalless international at Roker Park.

1957 Stan Anderson became the first England player to be sent off in an international when he was dismissed in Sofia playing for the U-23 side against Bulgaria.

1915 Sunderland AFC, heavily in debt due to the construction of a new stand and lack of income caused by WW1, advertised for people to take up a share offer or loan money to the club. It needed £4,000, in addition to a contribution from directors, to ensure the Club's survival past September 1915. (see September 18th)

MAY 20

2002 Striker Kevin Kyle made his full debut for Scotland; against South Africa in Hong Kong, before he had made his full debut for Sunderland.

1997 Ex-England winger Chris Waddle released, after only seven appearances for the club that he had supported as a boy, following Sunderland's relegation from the Premiership.

1987 Cameron Duncan and Steve Hetzke given free transfers to Motherwell and Chester City respectively.

1950 Sunderland beat Galatasary 4-3 in Istanbul during their first overseas tour following WW2.

Patrice Carteron

MAY 21

2001 French right back Patrice Carteron, remembered for his goal against Newcastle United, returned to St Etienne at the end of his two month loan spell.

1965 Ian McColl appointed Sunderland manager after resigning as Scotland manager.

1958 Goalkeeper Ronnie Routledge became the last player to be transferred from Sunderland to Bradford Park Avenue.

1953 Trevor Ford gained his final Welsh Cap as a Sunderland player, and scored both goals, in a 5-2 defeat in Yugoslavia.

MAY 22

1995 Peter Reid was confirmed as manager on a permanent basis after initially only getting the job until the end of the season. (see March 29th)

1967 Captain Colin Suggett became the first Sunderland player to collect the FA Youth Cup. Sunderland's youth team beat Birmingham City 1-0 in the second leg of the final at Roker Park to seal a 2-0 aggregate scoreline.

1959 Birth of striker Alan Brown in Easington. His son Chris later played for the Black Cats as well.

1950 Willie Watson became the first Sunderland player to be named in an England World Cup squad. Watson travelled to Brazil with the squad but did not make an appearance during the tournament.

MAY 23

1995 Paul Bracewell signed for Sunderland for a third spell; this time from Newcastle United for £50,000.

1976 Striker Mel Holden scored all five goals on Sunderland's South Seas post season tour in a 5-0 win over Tasmania.

1970 First competitive game in which Sunderland used two substitutes. Ritchie Pitt and Bruce Stuckey came on for Brian Heslop and Dennis Tueart in the Anglo Italian Cup game at Fiorentina.

1942 Sunderland met Wolverhampton Wanderers at Roker Park in the War League Cup final; the wartime replacement for the FA Cup. The first leg ended 2-2 courtesy of goals from Raich Carter and guest player Albert Stubbins. (see May 30th)

MAY 24

2009 Ricky Sbragia stood down as Sunderland manager following their 3-2 home defeat to Chelsea. However The Lads avoided relegation at the expense of their local rivals, Newcastle United, who lost 1-0 at Aston Villa.

1985 Following relegation to Division Two Len Ashurst was sacked as manager with Frank Burrows taking over in a caretaker role. (see July 11th)

1951 Keith Coleman, Sunderland's 1969 FA Youth Cup winning captain, born in Washington.

1947 Sunderland beat Brentford 2-1 in the final match of the much prolonged season making it the latest date on which they have played a League fixture. The cause was a severe winter that had led to numerous postponements.

MAY 25

1998 Sunderland lost 7-6 on penalties in the Division One play off final at Wembley following a 4-4 draw after extra time. There were differing emotions for two Sunderland born players; Clive Mendonca scored a hat trick for Charlton Athletic whilst Michael Gray missed the 14th penalty of the day.

1965 Legendary Scottish international Jim Baxter became Sunderland's record signing when he joined from Glasgow Rangers for £72,500.

1918 Birth of Cyril Brown in Ashington. He scored five goals for The Lads in his six appearances; all in the 1945-46 FA Cup games.

1880 Birth of Britain's first £1,000 player, Alf Common, in Millfield, Sunderland.

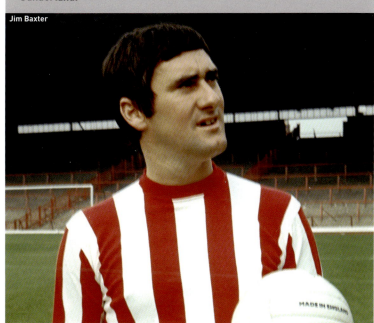
Jim Baxter

MAY 26

1989 Death of former Sunderland player, and manager of the defeated 1973 Leeds United FA Cup team, Don Revie, aged 61 from motor neurone disease.

1984 First of eight successive evening performances by American evangelist preacher Billy Graham at Roker Park.

1977 Gary Rowell became the first Sunderland player to represent England at U-21 level. He came on as a substitute to play alongside midfielder Peter Reid in a 1-0 win over Finland in Helsinki.

1957 Birth of winger Clive Walker in Oxford who became the first player to miss a penalty in a League Cup final. (see March 24th)

26.05.1984 Billy Graham

MAY 27

2009 Texan businessman Ellis Short increased his stake in Sunderland AFC from 30% to 100% thus taking control from the Drumaville Consortium. Niall Quinn remained as Chairman of the club. (see July 27th).

1985 Death of former half back and coach for Sunderland, Arthur Wright, aged 65.

1978 Sunderland beat Kenyan First Division side Ranogi 3-0 in Mombasa during their first, and so far only, tour in Africa. Arnott, Lee and Rostron netted for The Lads in the third game of the four match tour.

1913 The Football Association suspended Sunderland's captain Charlie Thomson for the first month of the 1913-14 season as a result of incidents that occurred during that year's FA Cup final. Aston Villa centre forward, Harry Hampton, and the match referee, Mr Adams, received the same punishment.

MAY 28

2002 Irish international defender Phil Babb signed from Sporting Lisbon on a free transfer.

1990 A tremendous display by goalkeeper Tony Norman ensured that Sunderland only lost 1-0 in the Division Two play off final against Swindon Town. (see June 13th).

1925 Birth of Scottish international half back, George Aitken, in Lochgelly. After retiring from football he was a judge for the Sunderland Echo `Spot the Ball' competition for over twenty years.

1889 John Auld, Sunderland's first League captain, was signed from Third Lanark. He was a shoemaker by trade and was given a boot and shoe business when he signed for Sunderland.

Phil Babb

MAY 29

2003 Death of Welsh international centre forward Trevor Ford aged 79.

1943 Birth of Mick Buxton, Sunderland's manager from 1993 to 1995, in Corbridge. (see March 29th and November 26th)

1941 Death of Sunderland's first League goalkeeper, William Kirkley, aged 78.

1879 Birth of centre forward and former coach Billy Hogg in Hendon, Sunderland; one of the hat trick heroes in Sunderland's 9-1 win at Newcastle United in 1908. (see December 5th)

Trevor Ford

MAY 30

1987 Denis Smith appointed as manager, in place of caretaker Bob Stokoe, with the task of guiding Sunderland straight back up to Division Two following the play off defeat against Gillingham. (see May 17th)

1980 Reserve keeper Jim Montgomery watched from the substitutes' bench as former team mate Brian Clough masterminded Nottingham Forest's retention of the European Cup against SV Hamburg in Madrid.

1962 Birth of Reuben Agboola in Islington who later became Sunderland's first Nigerian International (he qualified because his father was Nigerian).

1942 Wolves beat Sunderland 4-1 in the War League Cup final second leg to win the trophy 6-3 on aggregate. (see May 23rd)

MAY 31

1991 Sunderland's Richard Ord and Brian Atkinson helped England U-21s beat USSR U-21s 2-1 in a tournament in Toulon, France.

1973 England schools international midfielder Brian Chambers transferred to Arsenal for £25,000 after almost eight years on Sunderland's books.

1909 George Holley scored twice for England as they thrashed Hungary 8-2 in Budapest.

1904 Scottish centre half Sandy McAllister transferred to Derby County on the same day as forward Alf Common and goalkeeper Albert Lewis were signed from Sheffield United for a combined fee of £500.

Brian Atkinson

JUNE 1

2004 Republic of Ireland striker Stephen Elliott signed from Manchester City for a fee that rose based on appearances, Sunderland promotion and an Irish Cap to £375,000.

2002 Three Sunderland players were involved in World Cup finals games; Sorensen for Denmark against Uruguay; Kilbane and McAteer for Eire against Cameroon. Cameroon's scorer, Patrick Mboma, had ended his loan spell with The Lads nineteen days earlier.

1964 Defender Colin Todd signed as an apprentice from Chester-le-Street boys club.

1909 George Holley scored twice for England in consecutive days; this time in an 8-1 victory over Austria in Vienna. On the same day Sunderland ended their first European tour with an 8-3 victory over Nuremburg. (see May 15th)

JUNE 2

1997 Midfielder Lee Clark signed from Newcastle United for £2.5 million.

1976 Sunderland came close to losing their unbeaten record in the final game of their South Seas tour. A crowd of 36,000 saw the Singapore national team take a 2-0 lead before a brace from `Pop' Robson levelled the game.

1972 Jack Ashurst became the first Sunderland player to make his debut in June. He played centre half in an Anglo-Italian Cup away tie against Atalanta that Sunderland lost 3-2 after being two goals up at half time.

1969 "The King" left Sunderland. Charlie Hurley moved to Bolton Wanderers on a free transfer after 400 appearances for The Lads.

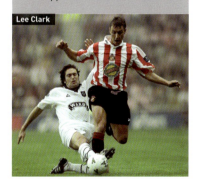
Lee Clark

JUNE 3

2009 Steve Bruce took the vacant Sunderland managerial position having earlier resigned from his position in charge of Wigan Athletic.

2005 Republic of Ireland striker Daryl Murphy signed from Waterford United for £100,000.

1999 Welsh international central defender Andy Melville moved to Fulham on a free transfer.

1889 Former Newcastle East End manager Tom Watson became Sunderland's first salaried team manager on a wage of 35 shillings per week.

Daryl Murphy

JUNE 4

2005 Goalkeeper Michael Ingham came on as a 77th minute substitute to make his Northern Ireland debut against Germany in Belfast only weeks before his Sunderland contract expired.

2000 Striker Niall Quinn captained Eire to a 2-2 draw against Mexico in a friendly in Chicago.

1972 Sunderland won an Anglo-Italian Cup away tie 3-1 against Cagliari in front of their second lowest post WW2 attendance for a first team game; 1,680. (see November 8th)

1896 Birth of outside right and WW1 Military Cross recipient Ted Clack in Highworth, Wiltshire.

Michael Ingham

JUNE 5

2003 Austrian goalkeeper Jurgen Macho moved to Chelsea on a free transfer.

2002 Niall Quinn came on as a substitute and set up a late equaliser as Eire drew 1-1 with Germany in the World Cup finals in Japan. The Irish team also contained Given, Breen, Harte Cunningham and Kilbane.

1999 Michael Gray came on for the second half of a goalless draw against Sweden becoming the first Sunderland player to appear for England at Wembley since Tony Towers in 1976. Stefan Schwarz played in Sweden's midfield during this game.

1955 Sunderland finished their post season American tour with a 2-2 draw against Huddersfield Town in Detroit. (see May 8th)

JUNE 6

2000 Kevin Phillips was named Carling Player of the Year after topping the Premiership scoring charts in his first season in the top flight.

1999 Peter Reid appointed England U-21 coach in addition to his managerial role at Sunderland.

1957 Birth of Sunderland's post WW2 penalty king, Gary Rowell, in Seaham.

1908 Arthur Bridgett became the first Sunderland player to score for England when he netted in a 6-1 win over Austria; England's first foreign opposition.

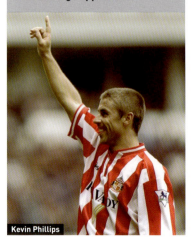
Kevin Phillips

JUNE 7

1999 Sunderland signed a £2 million three year sponsorship deal with Reg Vardy Ltd ending a fourteen year association with Vaux Breweries as the main club sponsor.

1981 Birth of centre forward Kevin Kyle in Stranraer.

1979 Ken Knighton promoted from first team coach to the position of manager.

1928 Birth of Ian McColl in Alexandria; Sunderland manager from 1965 to 1968.

Kevin Kyle

JUNE 8

1983 Future Scottish international Ally McCoist transferred to Glasgow Rangers for £200,000. (see August 26th)

1958 Sunderland winger Billy Bingham appeared in Northern Ireland's first World Cup finals game. This ended in a 1-0 victory over Czechoslovakia in Halmstad, Sweden.

1908 Arthur Bridgett scored in England's record victory outside of the British Isles; an 11-1 thrashing of Austria in Vienna.

1906 Death of John Campbell aged 36; the fastest player to score a century of goals for Sunderland. (see December 9th)

JUNE 9

1999 Niall Quinn's goal gave Eire a 1-1 draw against FYR Macedonia in Dublin, Allan Johnston scored in Scotland's 3-2 defeat against the Czech Republic in Prague and Michael Gray made his third, and final, England appearance against Bulgaria in Sofia. All of these games were Euro 2000 qualifiers.

1985 Midfielder Peter Reid made his England debut as a substitute for Ray Wilkins in a 1-0 defeat against Mexico in Mexico City.

1963 Charlie Hurley played and Ambrose Fogarty came on as a late first half substitute in Eire's first ever win over Scotland; 1-0 in Dublin.

1887 Birth of pre-WW1 centre forward John Cowell in Blyth.

JUNE 10

2006 Dwight Yorke, Stern John and Carlos Edwards appeared in Trinidad & Tobago's first World Cup finals game in the summer prior to joining Sunderland. The game in Dortmund ended in a goalless draw with Sweden.

2005 Defender Nyron Nosworthy joined Sunderland from Gillingham.

1982 Centre forward Tom Ritchie transferred to Bristol City after less then two seasons with The Lads.

1933 Birth of England international outside left Colin Grainger in Havercroft, Wakefield.

Dwight Yorke and Stern John

JUNE 11

2002 Thomas Sorensen kept a clean sheet as Denmark beat World Cup holders France 2-0 in Incheon to set up a Quarter Final showdown with England.

2000 Niall Quinn equalled the Republic of Ireland goalscoring record with his 20th international goal. It came in a 2-1 victory over South Africa in New York's Giants Stadium.

1996 Midfielder Alex Rae signed from Millwall for £1 million.

1953 Scottish international goalkeeper James Cowan signed from Greenock Morton for £16,000.

JUNE 12

1981 Former Stoke City manager Alan Durban appointed as Sunderland manager with caretaker Mick Docherty stepping down to become first team coach.

1976 Birth of Sunderland's first Danish player, Thomas Sorensen, in Fredericia.

1902 Death of Sunderland captain Matthew Ferguson from pleuro-pneumonia aged 26.

1878 Birth of 1912-13 League Championship and FA Cup runners up captain Charles Bellany Thomson in Prestonpans, near Edinburgh.

Thomas Sorensen

JUNE 13

2005 England U-21 striker Jon Stead signed from Blackburn Rovers for £1.8 million.
(see April 1st)

1990 The Football League refused Swindon Town's promotion to Division One as they had incurred thirty six breaches of League rules. As a result Sunderland were promoted in their place even though they had lost the play off final. (see May 28th)

1975 England international centre half Dave Watson transferred to Manchester City for £275,000.

1963 Former Sunderland player turned singer, Colin Grainger, appeared on the same bill as The Beatles at the Southern Sporting Club in Manchester.

JUNE 14

2006 Sunderland's longest serving chairman, Bob Murray, announced his resignation, effective June 30th, after twenty years in the position.

2005 Goalkeeper Kelvin Davis recruited from Ipswich Town for £1.25 million.

1955 Birth of Sunderland's youngest outfield player, Jimmy Hamilton, in Glasgow,
(see September 25th)

1933 Birth of 1960s outside right Harry Hooper in Pittington, County Durham.

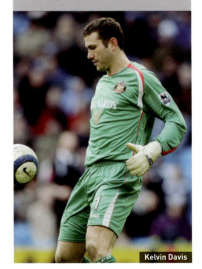
Kelvin Davis

JUNE 15

2006 Dwight Yorke, Carlos Edwards, Stern John and Kenwyne Jones played in Trinidad & Tobago's 2-0 defeat by England in the World Cup finals in Nuremburg.

2002 Thomas Sorensen conceded three first half goals as England eliminated Denmark in the second round of the World Cup finals in Niigata, Japan.

1979 Bryan `Pop' Robson signed from West Ham United for £45,000. This was the second of three occasions that he signed for The Lads. (see June 18th and July 28th)

1973 Birth of Norwegian international centre forward Tore Andre Flo in Stryn. (see August 30th)

JUNE 16

2002 Kevin Kilbane and David Connolly had their penalties saved in the shoot out as the Republic of Ireland were eliminated by Spain in the second round of the World Cup finals in Suwon, South Korea.

1989 Paul Hardyman signed from Portsmouth for £130,000.

1972 Full back Cec Irwin transferred to Yeovil Town to take up a player manager role.

1889 Birth of 1913 League Championship winning half back Francis Cuggy in Walker, Newcastle.

16/06/2002

JUNE 17

1974 Bobby Moncur signed from Newcastle United for £30,000.

1958 Billy Bingham played for Northern Ireland in a World Cup finals group play off game against Czechoslovakia to determine which team went through to the quarter final stage. Bingham's team won the game, held in Malmo, Sweden, by two goals to one.

1954 Ex-Sunderland forward Ivor Broadis scored twice for England in a 4-4 draw with Belgium in a World Cup finals game in Basle.

1953 Welsh international Ray Daniel signed from Arsenal for £28,000.

JUNE 18

2004 Right back Simon Ramsden, the player with the shortest Sunderland career in minutes, signed for Grimsby Town having been released by the Club. (see January 24th)

1974 Bryan `Pop' Robson signed from West Ham United for £145,000. This was the first of three occasions that he signed for The Lads. (see June 15th and July 28th)

1971 Birth of midfielder Jason McAteer in Birkenhead.

1911 John George "Tim" Coleman transferred to Fulham after scoring 21 goals in 33 appearances in his only season at Roker Park.

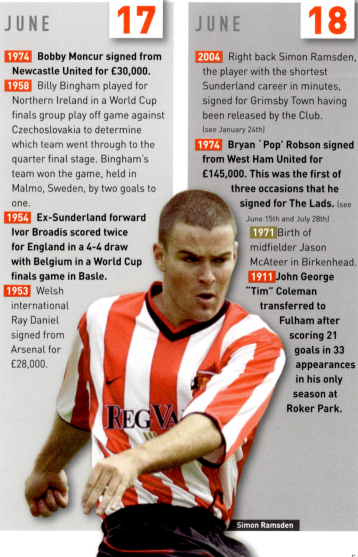
Simon Ramsden

JUNE 19

1998 Sunderland City Council bought the medal collection of the late Raich Carter for £30,000 on the day before it was due to be auctioned at Christies in Glasgow.

1983 Nick Pickering made his only England appearance in a 1-1 draw with Australia in Melbourne.

1975 Sunderland signed centre half Jeff Clarke from Manchester City for £100,000.

1958 Billy Bingham became the first Sunderland player to appear in a World Cup quarter final; Northern Ireland lost the game 4-0 to France in Norrkoping, Sweden.

Nick Pickering

JUNE 20

1968 Death of 1950s goalkeeper James Cowan aged 42.

1964 Birth of goalkeeper Alec Chamberlain in March, Lincolnshire.

1956 Birth of Peter Reid in Huyton; Sunderland's manager from 1995 to 2002.

1908 England forward Arthur Brown signed from Sheffield United for a world record fee of £1,600. (see April 6th)

Peter Reid

JUNE 21

2004 Midfielder Dean Whitehead signed from Oxford United for an appearance based fee that increased to £325,000.

2002 Claudio Reyna's World Cup ended as USA lost 1-0 to Germany in a World Cup quarter final in Ulsan, South Korea.

1997 International asset consultants, Henry Butcher & Co. Ltd, staged an auction of Roker Park artefacts at the ground as part of Sunderland's preparation for the move to their new stadium.

1928 Death of Edwardian era Irish international defender David English McConnell.

JUNE 22

2005 Shotton Colliery born Sunderland fan Tommy Miller joined The Lads on a free transfer from Ipswich Town.

1986 Butcher, Reid and Waddle, all with future connections with the Black Cats, played in England's 2-1 "Maradona hand of God" World Cup quarter final defeat against Argentina in Mexico City.

1966 Martin Harvey played for Northern Ireland in their 4-1 friendly victory over Mexico in Belfast.

1948 Birth of defender Colin Waldron in Manchester.

Tommy Miller

JUNE 23

- **1999** Sunderland gained permission from the City Council to increase the capacity of the Stadium of Light. (see March 1st and June 28th)
- **1987** David Bowie brought his Glass Spider World Tour to Roker Park. The concert will be remembered by those that attended for the incessant rain and Bowie's opening remark of "Hello Newcastle".
- **1953** England forward and future Sunderland manager, Billy Elliott, signed from Burnley for £26,000.
- **1923** Birth of post WW2 goalkeeper Robert Robinson in Newbiggin, Northumberland.

The Stadium of Light, prior to expansion

JUNE 24

- **1976** Death of 1930s centre forward Harry Bedford aged 76.
- **1933** Norwich City signed Sunderland forward Ted Vinall.
- **1931** Outside right George Robinson transferred to Charlton Athletic for £650.
- **1870** Birth of James Logan in Troon. He only played two games for the club as it is alleged he refused to play in the second team so was transferred back to Ayr.

JUNE 25

- **2004** Striker Tommy Smith signed for Derby County after being released by Sunderland at the end of the season.
- **1982** Billy Bingham's Northern Ireland team beat hosts Spain 1-0 in Valencia to progress to the second phase of the World Cup tournament.
- **1969** Colin Suggett became the first Sunderland player to move for a six figure sum when he joined West Bromwich Albion for £100,000.
- **1960** Death of legendary Sunderland goalscorer Charlie Buchan aged 68. After retiring from football he moved into journalism and founded the Football Monthly magazine in September 1951.

JUNE 26

- **2009** Sunderland Chairman Niall Quinn officially launched Sunderland's bid to stage World Cup games should England be awarded the 2018 competition.
- **1990** Future Sunderland player manager Terry Butcher and Chris Waddle helped England to a 1-0 extra time victory over Belgium in Bologna that took them through to the last eight of the World Cup.
- **1957** Manager Bill Murray stood down from the post as a result of the enquiry into illegal player payments at the club. (see January 7th, April 10th, April 25th and May 17th)
- **1954** Ex-Sunderland forward Ivor Broadis was in the England team that lost 4-2 to Uruguay in a World Cup quarter final game in Basle.

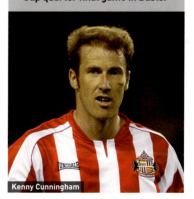
Kenny Cunningham

JUNE 27

2004 Scottish central defender Steven Caldwell joined the Black Cats from Newcastle United on a free transfer.
2001 Former French international striker Lilian Laslandes signed from Bordeaux for £3.5 million.
1967 Goalkeeper Sandy McLaughlan transferred to Kilmarnock for £2,500.
1944 Death of Edwardian era forward Arthur Brown aged 59. (see June 20th).

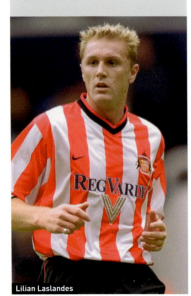
Lilian Laslandes

JUNE 28

1999 Sunderland announced a £6 million extension to the North Stand at the Stadium of Light that would provide an extra 6,000 seats for the start of the 2000-01 season. (see March 1st and June 23rd)
1993 Former captain Ian Atkins appointed assistant manager to Terry Butcher.
1955 Birth of England international forward, Eric Gates, in Ferryhill.
1911 Goalkeeper Walter Scott signed from Everton for £750. He is the only Sunderland player to have his contract terminated due to "palpable inefficiency".

Eric Gates

JUNE 29

2006 Death of 1964 promotion winning half back Jimmy McNab aged 66.
1995 Bryan 'Pop' Robson replaced Jimmy Montgomery as youth team coach.
1983 Midfielder Paul Bracewell signed for Sunderland, the first of three occasions, from Stoke City for £225,000.
1974 Northern Ireland international forward Tom Finney signed from Luton Town for £70,000.

JUNE 30

2004 Liam Lawrence signed from Mansfield Town for an appearance based fee that rose to £325,000.
1969 Former England international centre forward Joe Baker signed from Nottingham Forest for £30,000.
1931 1930s League Championship and FA Cup winning half back Charles Morgan Thomson signed from Glasgow Pollock.
1876 Birth of Scottish international right back Andrew McCombie in Inverness.

Liam Lawrence

JULY

JULY 1

2003 French forward David Bellion moved to Manchester United for a fee set by a tribunal at £2 million after he had refused to sign a new contract at Sunderland.

1985 Chris Turner transferred to Manchester United for a Sunderland record equalling fee of £275,000.

1980 Centre half Sam Allardyce signed from Bolton Wanderers for £150,000.

1914 Birth of John Feenan in Newry, County Down; the first Sunderland player to be capped by the Republic of Ireland; against Switzerland in Bern on May 17th 1937.

David Bellion

JULY 2

2002 Sunderland's reported record transfer fee bid of £9 million for Leeds United's Robbie Keane came to nothing as the player rejected the move to the Stadium of Light.

1998 Danish goalkeeper Thomas Sorensen signed from OB Odense for £1 million.

1979 Chris Turner signed from Sheffield Wednesday for £100,000.

1925 Sunderland sold their record League scorer Charlie Buchan to Arsenal for the unusual fee of £2,000 plus £100 for every goal he scored in the following season. He scored 21 times for Arsenal making the fee £4,100.

JULY 3

2006 A consortium led by former player Niall Quinn bought Sunderland for £10 million. Quinn replaced Bob Murray as Chairman.

1999 Sunderland signed former England international central defender Steve Bould from Arsenal for £400,000. Unfortunately his career was cut short after only fourteen months with the Black Cats due to a toe injury.

1984 Death of 1920s outside left Billy Death aged 83.

1959 Billy Elliott left Sunderland on a free transfer to join non-League Wisbech Town. He returned to Roker Park in January 1968 in a coaching capacity.

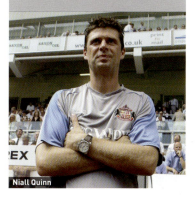

Niall Quinn

JULY 4

2000 Winger Sam Aiston moved to Shrewsbury Town on a free transfer.

1999 Sunderland's Player of the Century, Charlie Hurley, was awarded an honorary fellowship of Sunderland University.

1954 Birth of Malcom Crosby in South Shields; Sunderland's manager between 1991 and 1993.

1912 Former Sunderland amateur goalkeeper Ronald Brebner won an Olympic Gold medal in Stockholm when Great Britain beat Denmark 4-2 in the football final.

Malcolm Crosby

JULY 5

1997 Sunderland announced their intention to play all of the following season's reserve team games at New Ferens Park, Durham, in order to preserve the new Stadium of Light pitch. This was the first time that any Sunderland side would play a whole season outside the city boundary.

1996 Division One Championship winning keeper Alec Chamberlain transferred to Watford for £40,000.

1984 Central defender Rob Hindmarch moved to Derby County on a free transfer after spending seven years at Roker Park and Steve Berry joined The Lads, also on a free transfer, from Portsmouth.

1937 Midlander Cyril Hornby returned to his roots when he moved from Sunderland to become player manager of Birmingham League team Okengates Town.

JULY 6

2003 Midfielder Claudio Reyna made his comeback from a serious knee ligament injury, playing the final half hour, in USA's 2-0 victory over Paraguay in Ohio.

1995 Huddersfield Town signed Welsh international goalkeeper, Tony Norman, from Sunderland on a free transfer.

1990 Central defender Michael Heathcote transferred to Shrewsbury Town for £55,000.

1979 Frank Clark joined Sunderland from Nottingham Forest as Ken Knighton's assistant manager.

Claudio Reyna

JULY 7

1999 Midfielder Lee Clark transferred to Fulham for a Sunderland record fee of £3 million. (see July 23rd)

1997 Forward Paul Stewart, who had been the subject of two million pound transfers earlier in his career, signed for Stoke City after being released on a free transfer by Sunderland.

1993 Sunderland born centre forward Mick Harford transferred to Coventry City for £200,000 and on the same day Ian Rodgerson signed from Birmingham City for £140,000.

1941 Birth of Alan Durban in Port Talbot; Sunderland manager from 1981 to 1984.

JULY 8

2002 Irish midfielder Sean Thornton signed from Tranmere Rovers for an initial £225,000 fee plus additional appearances based payments.

2001 Julio Arca and new signing Nicolas Medina helped Argentina to a 3-0 victory over John Mensah's Ghana in the U-20 World Cup final in their home country.

1988 Former Scottish international full back George Burley moved to Gillingham on a free transfer.

1976 Birth of Talal El Karkouri in Casablanca; Sunderland's first Moroccan player.

Talal El Karkouri

JULY 9

2003 Lilian Laslandes ended his unsuccessful spell on Wearside with a transfer to OGC Nice.

1999 German international central defender Thomas Helmer became the first Sunderland player to be signed under the Bosman rule when he moved to Wearside from Bayern Munich.

1992 Scottish forward John Colquhoun signed from Millwall for £200,000.

1967 Sunderland, playing as Vancouver Royal Canadians, ended their North American tour with a 3-1 victory over Stoke City in Vancouver.

Thomas Helmer

JULY 10

1998 Central defender Paul Butler signed from Bury for £900,000.

1976 Striker Vic Halom transferred to Oldham Athletic for £25,000.

1927 Birth of 1950s forward Don Revie in Middlesbrough. After retiring from playing he became Leeds United's manager and was in that role when Sunderland beat them in the 1973 FA Cup final.

1919 Charles Bellany Thomson, Sunderland's pre-WW1 captain, retired after making 264 appearances for the Black Cats.

Don Revie at Wembley in 1973

JULY 11

2005 Sean Thornton transferred to Doncaster Rovers for £175,000.

1990 Future Sunderland captain and caretaker manager, Kevin Ball, signed from Portsmouth for £350,000.

1985 Ex-Southampton manager Lawrie McMenemy appointed as Sunderland manager with Frank Burrows ending his spell as caretaker manager.

1935 Birth of late 1950s keeper John Bollands in Middlesbrough.

Kevin Ball

JULY 12

1996 Tony Coton signed in a player coach capacity from Manchester United for £600,000. On the same day midfielder Gordon Armstrong moved to Bury on a free transfer after thirteen years at Roker Park.

1984 Centre forward Lee Chapman transferred to Sheffield Wednesday for £100,000.

1979 Sunderland agreed a Club record fee of £250,000 with NZ Zagreb for Yugoslav international striker Bozidar Bakota. However the deal fell through when he failed to get a work permit.

1927 Birth of 1950s forward, Charlie "Cannonball" Fleming, in Blairhall, Fife.

JULY 13

2007 Striker Michael Chopra signed from Cardiff City for a fee rising to £5 million based on appearances and team performance.

1994 Polish right back Dariusz Kubicki signed from Aston Villa for £100,000 following a successful two month loan spell on Wearside at the end of the previous season.

1984 Welsh international outside left Leighton James moved to Bury on a free transfer.

1966 Roker Park staged its first ever World Cup game; 30,956 spectators turned up to see Italy beat Chile 2-0.

JULY 14

2004 Sunderland's pre-season friendly against Carolina Select All Stars in Raleigh, North Carolina, was abandoned early in the second half due to lightning.

2000 Scottish international midfielder, Don Hutchison, signed from Everton for £2.5 million. Goalkeeper Jurgen Macho was signed from First Vienna on the same day.

1981 Full back Joe Bolton transferred to Middlesbrough for £200,000.

1961 Sunderland broke their transfer record to secure the signing of centre forward Brian Clough from Middlesbrough for £48,000.

JULY 15

2003 His Royal Highness the Duke of York officially opened the Academy of Light.

1999 Scorer of the final goal at Roker Park John Mullin signed for Burnley on a free transfer after being released by Sunderland. (see May 13th)

1997 Striker Kevin Phillips signed from Watford for £525,000. He made an immediate impact by scoring a post WW2 record 35 goals in his first season at the Club.

1967 Birth of Gordon Armstrong in Newcastle; the last midfielder to score over fifty goals for Sunderland.

13.07.1966

JULY 16

2000 An English U-16 international level record crowd of 21,061 saw Brazil beat England 2-1 at the Stadium of Light.

1994 Future Sunderland midfielder Stefan Schwarz helped Sweden beat Bulgaria 4-0 in the World Cup finals 3rd / 4th Play Off game in Los Angeles.

1966 USSR beat Italy 1-0 at Roker Park in a World Cup finals group game in front of 31,989 spectators.

1919 Pre-WW1 England international, George Holley, transferred to Brighton & Hove Albion.

JULY 17

1992 Midfielder Shaun Cunnington signed from Grimsby Town for £650,000.

1990 Former England forward, Peter Davenport, signed from Middlesbrough for £300,000.

1981 Death of 1930s outside right, Bert Davis, aged 74.

1940 Birth of centre forward Joe Baker in Liverpool. He appeared for Scotland at schoolboy level before being capped at U-23 and Full international levels for England.

JULY 18

2006 A statue of The Messiah, Bob Stokoe, was unveiled by his daughter at the Stadium of Light. Bobby Kerr, 1973 FA Cup winning captain, and members of that team were also in attendance.

1999 Sunderland lost 3-1 at Ibrox in a pre-season testimonial for Glasgow Rangers player Ian Ferguson. Former player for both sides, Ally McCoist, took part in the half time penalty shoot out competition wearing a Sunderland strip; the only time he wore the traditional stripes as he played during the two "candy stripe" seasons.

1984 Future captain Gary Bennett signed from Cardiff City for £85,000 and winger Clive Walker signed from Chelsea for £75,000.

1922 Birth of centre forward, Ron Turnbull, in Newbiggin, Northumberland; the only Sunderland player to score four goals on his debut.
(see November 29th)

16.07.1966 Italy v USSR

JULY 19

2006 Irish international defender Kenny Cunningham signed from Birmingham City on a free transfer.

1993 Northern Ireland striker Phil Gray signed from Luton Town for £775,000.

1965 Inaugural meeting of Sunderland AFC Supporters' Association held at Roker Park.

1962 Birth of former England international midfielder, Paul Bracewell, in Heswall, Cheshire; one of only two players signed three times by Sunderland.

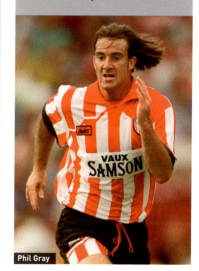
Phil Gray

JULY 20

2008 Sunderland started their pre-season friendlies with a 3-1 win over Sporting Lisbon in Albufiera thanks to goals from O'Donovan, Nosworthy and Stokes. However it prompted manager Roy Keane to question the term 'friendly' after Chopra was sent off and was sent to the stands for protesting the decision.

1975 A number of Sunderland's 1973 FA Cup winning team and former Black Cats Charlie Hurley, Len Shackleton and Ken Chisholm starred with Newcastle United and Middlesbrough players in a six-a-side cricket tournament in aid of autistic children at Durham's Chester-le-Street ground.

1973 Birth of former USA captain and midfielder, Claudio Reyna, in Livingston, New Jersey.

1966 Roker Park staged its final World Cup group game; USSR beat Chile 2-1 in front of 22,590 people.

JULY 21

2006 Kelvin Davis transferred to Southampton for £800,000 plus additional appearance based payments.

2004 Striker Darren Byfield moved to Gillingham on a free transfer.

1997 The Stadium of Light's new ticket office opened and immediately received more than 25,000 ticket enquiries for the opening game against Ajax.
(see July 30th)

1984 Sunderland played Nissan F.C. in a pre-season friendly to mark the announcement of the car manufacturer's decision to build a factory in Washington. The Lads' 5-2 victory at Roker Park included a Colin West hat trick.

JULY 22

1994 The Lads won 2-0 at Averoykamerateno, leaders of their Second Division, during a thirteen day pre-season tour of Norway. Craig Russell and Phil Gray got the second half goals.

1987 Sunderland born full back John Kay signed from Wimbledon for £22,500.

1984 Birth of loanee winger Stewart Downing in Middlesbrough.

1978 Centre forward Mel Holden transferred to Blackpool for £60,000.

JULY 23

1999 Sunderland received their record transfer fee when Michael Bridges was sold to Leeds United for £5 million.

1984 Striker `Pop' Robson ended this third and final playing spell with Sunderland when he moved to Carlisle United on a free transfer.

1966 Roker Park staged its only World Cup quarter final in which USSR beat Hungary 2-1 in front of 26,844 spectators.

1953 Goalkeeper Harry Threadgold transferred to Southend United for £3,500.

23.07.1966 Igor Chislenko scores Russia's first goal v Hungary

JULY 24

2003 Midfielder Gavin McCann transferred to Aston Villa for £2.25 million.
1998 Central defender Richard Ord transferred to Queens Park Rangers for £675,000.
1996 Steaua Bucharest were the visitors to Roker Park for Richard Ord's testimonial game. The Romanian side won 1-0 in front of only 8,808 people.
1958 Northern Irish international Billy Bingham transferred to Luton Town for £15,000.

Billy Bingham

JULY 25

2006 Chairman Niall Quinn appointed himself manager until he found the right manager for the Club. (see 28th August)
2000 Midfielder Julio Arca signed from Argentinos Juniors for £3.5 million.
1977 England international midfielder Tony Towers transferred to Birmingham City for £140,000.
1973 Birth of Sunderland's post WW2 leading goalscorer, Kevin Phillips, in Hitchin.

JULY 26

2006 Argentine U-21 international Julio Arca transferred to Middlesbrough for £1.75 million.
1983 Death of 1937 FA Cup final scorer Eddie Burbanks aged 70.
1977 Sunderland sold their 1973 FA Cup final goalscorer, Ian Porterfield, to Sheffield Wednesday for £20,000.
1936 Birth of Lawrie McMenemy in Gateshead; Sunderland's manager between 1985 and 1987.

JULY 27

2006 Niall Quinn and his Drumaville Group consortium formally completed their takeover of Sunderland Association Football Club.
2000 Slovakian international captain Stanislav Varga signed from Slovan Bratislava for £650,000.
1991 Reuben Agboola helped Nigeria qualify for the African Nations' Cup finals as they thrashed Burkina Faso 7-1 in Lagos.
1982 Midfielder Ian Atkins signed from Shrewsbury Town with striker Alan Brown moving in the opposite direction.

Julio Arca

JULY 28

1993 Gary Bennett's testimonial match against Glasgow Rangers attracted a crowd of 21,862 at Roker Park. Rangers won the game 3-1.

1988 Centre forward Keith Bertschin transferred to Walsall for £30,000. Bertschin scored both the first and last goals scored by Sunderland in the third tier of English football. (see August 15th and May 7th)

1983 Bryan 'Pop' Robson signed for the third time; this time as player coach from Chelsea on a free transfer.

1979 Gary Rowell was sent off early in the second half of a pre-season friendly in Lausanne, Switzerland. The game finished as a 1-1 draw.

JULY 29

2000 Portuguese TV showed live coverage of the Porto versus Sunderland pre-season friendly. The Portuguese side used this as a warm up for their upcoming Champions League qualifying games and came out victors by one goal to nil.

1999 Swedish international midfielder, Stefan Schwarz, signed from Valencia for a Sunderland record fee of £3.75 million.

1994 Bobby Robson's Portuguese side Porto were the visitors for long serving midfielder Gordon Armstrong's testimonial at Roker Park.

1982 Birth of Republic of Ireland midfielder Andy Reid in Dublin.

JULY 30

2007 The combined signings of Steed Malbranque, Pascal Chimbonda and Teemu Tainio from Tottenham Hotspur completed Sunderland's most expensive transfer deal.

1997 Rock group Status Quo arrived by helicopter as part of the pre-match entertainment for the opening game at the Stadium of Light, whose name had been revealed shortly after midnight by Chairman Bob Murray. The game, against Dutch side Ajax ended in a goalless draw.

1981 Scottish left back Iain Munro signed from Stoke City for £150,000.

1957 Alan Brown became Sunderland manager for the first of two occasions. (see February 9th)

JULY 31

2003 Central defender Jody Craddock transferred to Wolverhampton Wanderers for £1.75 million.

1999 Captain Kevin Ball brought Italian side Sampdoria to the Stadium of Light for his testimonial game.

1987 Central defender and penalty expert, John MacPhail, signed from Bristol City for £23,000.

1964 Manager Alan Brown resigned, just three weeks before Sunderland's return to the top flight, to join Sheffield Wednesday leaving the Club to be run by the directors. (see November 14th)

30.07.1997

AUGUST

AUGUST 1

2007 Sunderland's 4-0 pre-season friendly victory at Galway United included Michael Chopra's and Kieran Richardson's first goals for the club.

1997 Irish forward David Kelly transferred to Tranmere Rovers for £350,000.

1996 Northern Irish international Phil Gray became the first Sunderland player to move on free transfer under the recently created Bosman ruling when he joined French club Nancy.

1981 A 1-0 win at Heart of Midlothian in the first pre-season friendly saw Sunderland take to the field in their new "candy" striped tops and red shorts. This unpopular change only lasted for two seasons.

AUGUST 2

2005 Sunderland's most prolific goalscoring loan player, Anthony Le Tallec, was signed on a season long temporary contract from Liverpool.

1991 Future Welsh international midfielder John Cornforth transferred to Swansea City for an appearance based fee totalling £50,000.

1985 Eire international goalkeeper Seamus McDonagh signed on loan from Notts County.

1975 Sunderland lost 3-2 at Ayresome Park against Middlesbrough in their earliest first team competitive game of a season. Sunderland's scorers in their first ever Anglo-Scottish Cup tie were Denis Longhorn, with a penalty, and a debut goal by Tommy Gibb.

AUGUST 3

2001 Swiss international right back Bernt Haas signed from Grasshoppers Zurich for £750,000.

1974 Sunderland beat Newcastle United 2-1, in front of 28,738 spectators at Roker Park, in their first ever Texaco Cup tie. The game marked the debuts of Stan Ternent, Bobby Moncur, `Pop' Robson and Tom Finney. Future Sunderland left back Michael Gray was born on the same day in Castletown, Sunderland.

1950 Stalwart full back Jack Hedley signed from Everton for £10,000.

1929 1937 FA Cup winning centre half Robert Johnston signed from Alva Albion Rovers.

Anthony Le Tallec

AUGUST 4

2006 Goalkeeper Darren Ward signed from Norwich City on a free transfer.

1984 Sunderland retained the pre-season Isle of Man Trophy by beating Blackburn Rovers 1-0 in the final thanks to a Colin West goal. (see August 9th)

1979 Ken Knighton's first competitive game in charge ended in a 4-2 defeat at Gigg Lane in an Anglo-Scottish Cup tie against Bury.

1963 Birth of midfielder, and occasional left back, Nick Pickering in Newcastle.

Nick Pickering

AUGUST 5

2009 England international striker Darren Bent became Sunderland's record signing after moving north from Tottenham Hotspur for an initial fee of £10 million. The deal could see him eventually cost the club a reported £16.5 million.

1992 Sunderland celebrated becoming a city by staging a pre-season friendly with Tottenham Hotspur. Darren Anderton scored a hat trick for the visitors who ran out 3-0 winners in front of 22,672 people at Roker Park.

1978 Birth of Sunderland's most used substitute, 67 occasions, Michael Bridges in North Shields. (see January 22nd)

1958 Scottish teenage goalscoring sensation Nick Sharkey signed from St Patrick's High School, Dumbarton. In 1959-60 season he had the unusual distinction of appearing for Sunderland's junior, youth, reserve and first teams.

AUGUST 6

2006 Republic of Ireland central defender Kenny Cunningham made his debut in a 2-1 televised defeat at Coventry City. Niall Quinn's first game in charge was also the earliest date on which Sunderland have opened a League campaign.

1999 Forward Martin Smith signed for Sheffield United on a free transfer after almost nine years with the Black Cats.

1993 Welsh international central defender Andy Melville signed from Oxford United for £500,000 plus Anton Rogan moving in the opposite direction.

1973 The English and Scottish FA Cup winners met in a friendly at Parkhead with Sunderland coming out 2-1 victors over Celtic.

AUGUST 7

2007 Republic of Ireland U-21 forward Roy O'Donovan signed from Cork City.

2004 Stephen Elliott, Dean Whitehead and Liam Lawrence made their debuts in a 2-0 opening day defeat at Coventry City.

1999 Sunderland's unbeaten run of eighteen games came to an abrupt halt in their first game back in the Premiership. Steve Bould and Carsten Fredgaard made their debuts in the 4-0 defeat at Stamford Bridge.

1985 Striker Dave Swindlehurst signed from West Ham United for £80,000. A month later he scored Sunderland's first goal of the season. (see September 7th)

07.08.1999 Steve Bould

AUGUST 8

2007 Sunderland broke the British transfer record for a goalkeeper by signing Heart of Midlothian and Scotland keeper Craig Gordon for a fee that could rise to £9 million.

2003 Danish keeper Thomas Sorensen transferred to Aston Villa for £2.25 million.

1998 Midfielder Lee Clark broke his leg in the opening game of the season; a 1-0 home victory over Queens Park Rangers in which Sorensen and Paul Butler made their debuts.

1993 Ian Rodgerson, Phil Gray, Andy Melville and Derek Ferguson were involved in a car crash in Roker following a pre-season friendly at Middlesbrough. Rodgerson was the most seriously injured suffering a dislocated shoulder which significantly delayed his debut for The Lads.

Craig Gordon

AUGUST 9

2003 Sunderland kicked off their season at 5.35 pm in a televised game at Nottingham Forest. This is probably the hottest conditions in which they have played a competitive game as the pitchside temperature at kick off was 102°F (39°C).

1985 Former England international forward Eric Gates signed from Ipswich Town for £150,000.

1983 Sunderland beat St Mirren 1-0 in the final of the pre-season Isle of Man Trophy tournament.

1975 Centre forward Mel Holden made his debut in the first Anglo-Scottish Cup tie to be played at Roker Park. The game, in front of 12,673 spectators, ended in a 1-0 win for Carlisle United.

AUGUST 10

2005 Striker Andy Gray, son of former player Frank, signed from Sheffield United for £1.1 million.

2004 Sunderland's first home game of the season, and Steven Caldwell's debut, ended in a 3-1 victory over Crewe Alexandra courtesy of goals from Carl Robinson, Marcus Stewart and Stephen Elliott.

1999 The first Premiership game to be played at the Stadium of Light ended in 2-0 victory thanks to two second half Kevin Phillips goals against his former club Watford. It also marked the debuts of Stefan Schwarz and John Oster.

1971 Birth of ex-manager and former Republic of Ireland midfielder Roy Keane in Cork.

09.08.2003

AUGUST 11

2007 Debutant Michael Chopra came off the substitute's bench to net a last minute winner at home to Tottenham Hotspur in Sunderland's opening Premiership game of the season. This 1-0 Sky televised victory also marked the debuts of new signings Craig Gordon, Paul McShane, Dickson Etuhu and Kieran Richardson.

1998 Two first half Danny Dichio goals, his first for the Club, at Bootham Crescent sealed a first round first leg League Cup victory over York City.

1979 Chris Turner became the first Sunderland keeper to appear as a substitute, also his debut, when he replaced Barry Siddall at half time, a pre-arranged change, in a home Anglo-Scottish Cup tie against Oldham Athletic.

1967 Former Scottish international centre forward Ralph Brand signed from Manchester City for £5,000.

AUGUST 12

1995 Sunderland started their season at Roker Park with a 2-1 defeat against Leicester City. This proved to be the first of only two home defeats in that Division One Championship winning season.

1978 Gordon Chisholm and Ian Watson made their debuts in a 2-1 Anglo-Scottish Cup defeat at Sheffield United.

1961 New signing Brian Clough scored twice in a 3-0 win over Aarhus in a pre-season friendly at Roker Park. This gave him four goals in his first two appearances in red and white stripes.

1904 Goalkeeper Teddy Doig transferred to Liverpool for £150 after a then record 457 appearances and four Division One Championship medals.

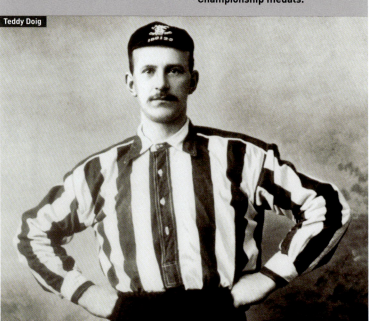

Teddy Doig

AUGUST 13

2005 Striker Andy Gray scored on his debut in a 3-1 opening day home defeat against Charlton Athletic. Sunderland's return to the Premiership also marked the debuts of Kelvin Davis, Tommy Miller, Jon Stead and Nyron Nosworthy.

2003 Sunderland's first round League Cup tie at Mansfield Town saw centre forward Kevin Kyle score for both sides in the final two minutes to turn an expected 1-0 Sunderland win into a 2-1 victory. This also marked Norwegian striker Tore Andre Flo's final game for the Black Cats.

1974 Former player Don Revie opened an exhibition entitled "A History of Sunderland AFC" at Sunderland Arts Centre.

1933 Birth of 1950s centre forward Don "The Rhino" Kichenbrand in Germiston, South Africa.

AUGUST 14

2003 Post WW2 record goalscorer Kevin Phillips transferred to Southampton for £3.25 million.

1997 Death of 1950s Scottish centre forward Charlie "Cannonball" Fleming aged 70.

1993 Sunderland suffered their worst start to a season with a 5-0 defeat at Derby County. This was the first League match that they were allowed to name three substitutes and also goalkeeper Alec Chamberlain's debut.

1971 Left back Bobby Park suffered a broken leg in a 1-1 draw with Birmingham City in front of Roker Park's lowest accurately recorded opening day crowd; only 9,749 turned up for the game played in pouring rain.

AUGUST 15

2002 Right back Stephen Wright signed from Liverpool for £3 million.

1997 Niall Quinn scored the first goal at the Stadium of Light, and Kevin Phillips netted on his debut, in a 3-1 win over Manchester City.

1996 Republic of Ireland centre forward Niall Quinn signed from Manchester City for £1.3 million on the same day that a time capsule containing Club memorabilia was buried on the construction site for the Stadium of Light.

1987 Keith Bertschin scored Sunderland's first ever goal in the third division of English football, in a 1-0 win at Brentford.

(see May 7th)

15.08.2002

AUGUST 16

2003 Michael Gray made his final Sunderland appearance, almost eleven years after his debut, in a 1-0 home defeat against Millwall which extended the Black Cats run of League defeats to seventeen.

1980 Central defender Sam Allardyce made his debut in Sunderland's first game back in the top flight; a 3-1 home victory over Everton.

1975 Chelsea were the visitors to Roker Park for the opening game of the season. Goals from `Pop' Robson and Denis Longhorn gave The Lads a 2-1 win.

1964 Birth of 1980s right back Barry Venison in Stanley, County Durham.

AUGUST 17

2002 The Lads kicked off their fourth consecutive season in the Premiership with a 0-0 draw at Ewood Park. This game saw the debuts of defenders Stephen Wright and Phil Babb.

1996 Tony Coton and Niall Quinn made their debuts in Sunderland's inaugural Premiership game; a goalless draw at home to Leicester City. This was also the first League game in which the Black Cats could name five substitutes.

1985 An expectant Roker Park crowd came to see Lawrie McMenemy's first game in charge. However the new strike force of Gates and Swindlehurst failed to deliver with The Lads losing 2-0 to Bobby Saxton's Blackburn Rovers.

(see September 7th)

1896 Sunderland's first manager, Tom Watson, left the club to become manger of Liverpool. Robert Campbell, centre forward John's half-brother, stepped up from `A' team secretary to take over the post.

AUGUST 18

2001 The Lads opened their campaign with a 1-0 home victory over Ipswich Town courtesy of a first half Kevin Phillips penalty. Right back Bernt Haas and striker Lilian Laslandes made their debuts in front of Sunderland's largest opening day home crowd for thirty nine years.

1973 Sunderland, FA Cup holders, met Tottenham Hotspur, League Cup holders, in a pre-season friendly at Roker Park. A crowd of over 22,000 saw both cups paraded at the start of the game which ended 1-0 to Spurs thanks to a goal from Eppleton born Ralph Coates.

1962 Over 48,000 turned out on the opening day of the season to see Sunderland beat Middlesbrough 3-1 thanks to goals from two Sunderland legends; a brace from Brian Clough and one from Charlie Hurley.

1951 Sunderland's 4-3 opening day win at The Baseball Ground was a multi-national effort. Each of the four goal scorers hailed from a different home country; Shackleton (England), McLain (Scotland), Bingham (Northern Ireland) and Ford (Wales).

18.08.2001

AUGUST 19

2003 Sunderland players Kevin Kilbane, Gary Breen and Colin Healy were capped for Eire against Australia in Dublin. On the same day future striker Stephen Elliott scored a hat trick, whilst on Manchester City's books, on his Eire U-21 debut against Poland in Gdansk.

2000 The extended North Stand was used for the first time in the opening day fixture against Arsenal. Niall Quinn scored the only goal but the game will be remembered for the inspired performances of debutants Stan Varga and second half substitute goalkeeper Jurgen Macho.

1999 Death of Sunderland's 1937 FA Cup winning goalkeeper, John Mapson, aged 82.

1961 Brian Clough scored on his debut at newly promoted Walsall in a 4-3 defeat. He virtually kept up this goal a game average in his short Sunderland career netting 63 times in 74 appearances.

AUGUST 20

2005 Central defender and ex-Evertonian Alan Stubbs made his Sunderland debut at Anfield. The game ended in a 1-0 defeat and saw Andy Welsh harshly sent off for a challenge on Liverpool's Luis Garcia.

1991 Sunderland convincingly won their first away game back in the second tier of English football. Owers, Armstrong and Pascoe scored in the 3-0 win over Barnsley.

1980 A goal from Stan Cummins and a second half John Hawley hat trick gave The Lads a 4-0 away victory at Manchester City. This win left newly promoted Sunderland heading the top flight; albeit after only two games of the season.

1936 Death of Scottish international full back William Agnew aged 55; the first person to play for all three major North East clubs.

AUGUST 21

2002 Matthew Piper joined Sunderland from Leicester City for £3.5 million. (see January 19th)

1996 Sunderland recorded their first victory in the Premiership; first half goals from Michael Gray, Niall Quinn (2) and Richard Ord sealed a 4-1 win at Nottingham Forest.

1965 Debut of Scottish international Jim Baxter in a 1-0 defeat at Elland Road.

1954 The Black Cats started their season in front of the club's highest home opening game attendance. The game against West Bromwich Albion attracted 56,827 even though "The Bank of England Club", as Sunderland were referred to by the press, had not bought anyone during the close season.

Jim Baxter

AUGUST 22

2003 Expensive signing Norwegian striker Tore Andre Flo ended his year long spell on Wearside with an undisclosed transfer fee move to Italian club Siena.

1998 Sunderland beat Tranmere Rovers 5-0 in their second home game of the season with Dichio netting his first League goals for the club.

1964 Debut of goalkeeper Derek Forster in Sunderland's first game back in the top flight; a 3-3 home draw against Leicester City. He became the youngest player to play for the club aged 15 years 185 days.

1947 Birth of 1973 FA Cup winning right back Dick Malone in Carfin, Lanarkshire.

Dick Malone

AUGUST 23

2006 Swedish international winger Tobias Hysen signed from Djurgardens for £1.7 million. His father, Glenn, played for Liverpool in the early 1990s.

2005 French player Anthony Le Tallec, on loan from Liverpool, could have had a hat trick in the first half of his debut at home to Manchester City. However he only converted one of his chances and the match ended in a 2-1 defeat.

2003 Sunderland finally ended a record run of seventeen consecutive League defeats with a 2-0 victory at Preston North End thus avoiding equalling the League's worst sequence, 18 games, held by Darwen since 1899.

1958 Colin Grainger scored Sunderland's first League goal outside of the top flight of English football in their inaugural Division Two game. The match at Lincoln City ended in a 3-1 defeat.

AUGUST 24

2004 Sunderland beat Chester City 3-0 in a first round League Cup tie in front of the Stadium of Light's lowest attendance for a first team game; 11,450 spectators.

1999 French midfielder Eric Roy signed from Olympique Marseille for £200,000.

1957 Inside forward Len Shackleton was injured in the opening fixture of the season against Arsenal at Roker Park and did not play in the second half. This was his final appearance for The Lads as he retired shortly afterwards due to a recurring ankle injury.

1955 Aston Villa were beaten 5-1 in the first home game of the season by Sunderland's "Bank of England" team starting a run of nine wins in eleven games that took them to the head of the top flight table.

Eric Roy

AUGUST 25

1999 Sunderland recorded their first away win of the season; 2-1 at St James' Park in what turned out to be Ruud Gullit's final game in charge of The Magpies.

1990 Former England striker Peter Davenport netted on his debut in a 3-2 defeat at Norwich City. This proved to be John MacPhail's last game for Sunderland and his only top flight appearance in a career of almost 600 English League games.

1984 Gary Bennett scored after two minutes of his debut in a 3-1 home victory over Southampton. This match also saw the debuts of Steve Berry, Howard Gayle and Clive Walker.

1951 "Clown Prince of Soccer" Len Shackleton netted his only Sunderland hat trick in a 3-0 home victory over Manchester City.

AUGUST 26

2001 A Kevin Phillips strike ensured that The Lads stretched their unbeaten run of Premiership games at Newcastle United to four games with a 1-1 draw in Don Hutchison's final appearance in red and white stripes.

1981 Teenage Scottish striker Ally McCoist signed from St Johnstone for a Sunderland record fee of £355,000. The fee was not fully paid as he moved to Glasgow Rangers after only two seasons on Wearside. (see June 8th)

1939 Sunderland opened the season with a 3-0 home victory over Derby County. This game, and the further two games played, were all expunged from record books when WW2 forced the abandonment of the League programme. (see September 2nd)

1914 Birth of Alan Brown in Corbridge; the man who managed Sunderland on two separate occasions; 1957 to 1964 and 1968 to 1972.

AUGUST 27

2005 Sunderland conceded their fastest ever penalty; after 12 seconds of the match at Wigan Athletic. Jason Roberts converted the spot kick for the only goal of the game.

1988 The Black Cats started their League programme with a 1-1 draw in their first ever game against Bournemouth. This was the only opening game of the season in the 1980s in which Sunderland did not field a debutant.

1958 Right winger Clive Bircham scored Sunderland's first ever home League goal outside the top flight of English football in a 2-1 defeat by Fulham.

1942 Death of former England forward and Sunderland's fourth highest goal scorer George Holley aged 56.

AUGUST 28

2006 Roy Keane appointed as the new Sunderland manager. He watched from the West Stand as The Lads finally gave outgoing manager Niall Quinn his first, and only, win; 2-0 over West Bromwich Albion. This game was also Toby Hysen's debut.

2002 A Jason McAteer goal gave Sunderland all of the points at Elland Road in what proved to be their only League victory away from home all season.

1990 This warm Tuesday evening opening home fixture saw Kevin Ball make his Sunderland debut in a goalless draw against a Tottenham Hotspur side containing two of England's World Cup heroes. However the receptions for Gary Lineker and ex-Magpie Paul Gascoigne were markedly different.

1982 Sunderland are Champions of Europe!! Goals from Colin West, Ally McCoist and Nick Pickering gave the Black Cats a 3-1 win at European Cup holders Aston Villa in the first game of the season.

AUGUST 29

2003 USA captain Claudio Reyna transferred to Manchester City for £2.5 million on the same day that Emerson Thome moved to Bolton Wanderers on a free transfer.

1981 Ally McCoist, Iain Munro and Nick Pickering made their debuts in an opening day 3-3 draw at Ipswich Town. Substitute McCoist made an immediate impact setting up Mick Buckley's second goal with a deft back heel to put Sunderland 3-1 up.

1928 Sunderland benefited from two own goals for the only time in their history; Jones and Whyte of Blackburn Rovers turned the ball into their own net in a 3-1 home win.

1925 David Halliday scored two goals on his Sunderland debut at Birmingham. He went on to score ten goals in his first four games for The Lads.

AUGUST 30

2002 Tore Andre Flo signed from Glasgow Rangers for a Club record fee of £6.75 million and Marcus Stewart signed from Ipswich Town for £1.5 million on the eve of the newly imposed early season transfer deadline.

1978 Bobby Kerr, Sunderland's 1973 FA Cup winning captain, made his final appearance for the Black Cats in a 2-0 second round League Cup home defeat to Stoke City.

1958 Sunderland picked up their first points outside of the top flight with a 2-1 home victory over Liverpool. The Lads had to wait another 24 games and over 44 years for the next home League win over Liverpool.

(see December 15th)

1919 Charlie Buchan scored the first goal for Sunderland on the resumption of League football after WW1. This game, a 2-1 home win over Aston Villa, was also The Black Cats first ever League game played in August.

AUGUST 31

2006 New manager Roy Keane immediately delved into the transfer market on deadline day signing six players; David Connolly, Graham Kavanagh, Liam Miller, Stan Varga, Ross Wallace and Dwight Yorke.

2002 Norwegian striker Tore Andre Flo scored on his debut in a 1-1 draw with Manchester United. Towards the end of the game Eire international and future Sunderland manager Roy Keane was sent off, for the eleventh time in his career, for elbowing fellow Irish international Jason McAteer.

2000 Brazilian centre back Emerson Thome was signed from Chelsea for a Sunderland record fee of £4.5 million.

1946 League football resumed after a seven year break caused by WW2. Roker Park witnessed the unusual sight of Raich Carter leading out the opposition, as captain of Derby County, following his wartime move to the Baseball Ground. Sunderland won the game 3-2 in front of 48,466 thanks to a Burbanks penalty and a brace from Cliff Whitelum.

Tore Andre Flo

SEPTEMBER 1

1990 A late Gary Bennett goal sealed a dramatic 2-1 home victory over Manchester United giving Sunderland their first top flight win since April 1985.

1979 A Club record fourteen League match unbeaten run away from Roker Park ended with a 3-0 defeat at Oldham Athletic.

1956 Sunderland's third home game of the season produced their best win since Boxing Day 1934. Charlton Athletic were thrashed 8-1 thanks to John Hannigan's only hat trick for The Lads, a brace from Len Shackleton and one each from Daniel, Anderson and Fleming.

1894 The Sunderland versus Derby County game ended up as a game of three halves. The match started with a linesman in control as the referee was delayed. He arrived at half time and ordered the game to restart. Sunderland won the game 8-0 having led 3-0 at the end of both first halves.

SEPTEMBER 2

1964 A crowd of 52,177 turned up to see Brian Clough's return to action twenty months after damaging his cruciate ligaments. This home game, against West Bromwich Albion, ended in a 2-2 draw thanks to goals from Mulhall and Hurley.
(see December 26th)

1939 The Football League was suspended following this Saturday's games due to the outbreak of WW2. Arsenal's centre forward Ted Drake scored four times in a 5-2 win over The Lads however all three games at the start of this season were later expunged from the records.

1936 The rebuilt 15,500 capacity Archibald Leitch designed Clockstand was officially opened by Lady Raine before the 3-2 home win against Derby County.

1907 The first ever Sunderland match day programme was produced for the match against Manchester City. Previously only a teamsheet had been issued.

SEPTEMBER 3

1994 A first half Phil Gray strike gave Sunderland a 1-1 draw against Wolverhampton Wanderers meaning all three home games of the season so far had been drawn.

1977 Forward Billy Hughes transferred to Derby County for £30,000 following a one month loan spell with The Rams.

1966 Neil Martin scored a hat trick in a 4-0 top flight home victory over Blackpool.

1892 Sunderland started the defence of their first top flight Championship with a 6-0 away win at Accrington.

Alex Rae

SEPTEMBER 4

1996 Scottish midfielder Alex Rae made his debut, as a substitute for Steve Agnew, in a 2-1 home defeat to Newcastle United. Sunderland had taken a first half lead thanks to a Martin Scott penalty.

1974 Sunderland forward Tom Finney scored after only three minutes of his Northern Ireland debut; in Oslo against Norway.

1942 Birth of 1960s forward Willie McPheat in Caldercruix, Scotland.

1933 Len Duns signed for Sunderland from Newcastle West End. His playing appearances for The Lads were reduced due to WW2 however his Roker career still extended until May 1952.

SEPTEMBER 5

2000 Left sided Argentine midfielder Julio Arca scored on his debut at home to West Ham United in a 1-1 draw. The game was also Brazilian Emerson Thome's first for Sunderland.

1997 First half goals from Michael Gray, Lee Clark, Kevin Phillips and Allan Johnston were enough to give The Lads a 4-0 victory at Bradford City. This started a run of five successive victories at Valley Parade during which Sunderland scored 17 goals.

1979 Sunderland beat Newcastle United 7-6 on penalties in the League Cup second round second leg game at St James' Park. Both legs had finished in 2-2 draws. This was the first time the Black Cats had settled a drawn competitive game in this manner.

1925 Silksworth born record goal scorer Bobby Gurney scored nine goals on his debut for Sunderland Reserves in a 14-0 win over Hartlepool Reserves.

SEPTEMBER 6

1988 A brace each from Marco Gabbiadini, against his former club, and Colin Pascoe gave Sunderland a comfortable 4-0 victory over York City in a League Cup first round second leg game at Roker Park.

1967 Defending League champions Manchester United were held 1-1 at Roker Park thanks to a Colin Suggett goal. This was the fifth consecutive game in which he had scored.

1965 Allan Gauden replaced the injured Mike Hellawell thus becoming the first substitute to be used by Sunderland. This game at Villa Park was also Gauden's debut for The Lads.

1930 Debut of 1930s captain Alex Hastings in a 1-1 draw at Portsmouth. He later emigrated to Australia and was awarded the British Empire Medal in 1981 for his work as president of South Australia's Soccer Federation.

SEPTEMBER 7

1985 David Swindlehurst finally scored Sunderland's first goal of the season in their sixth game; a 3-3 draw at home to Grimsby Town. The 494 minutes goal drought remains Sunderland's worst start to a season.

1974 A Billy Hughes hat trick helped Sunderland to a 5-1 demolition of Bristol Rovers and maintained their 100% home start to the season.

1929 Roker Park's new Grandstand was officially opened before the home game against Manchester City. This 10,000 capacity stand, designed by Archibald Leitch and famous for its iron latticework, had cost £35,000 to construct. Sunderland won the game 5-2 with David Halliday scoring his 12th, and final, hat trick for The Lads.

1896 Sunderland drew 1-1 at Burnley in a Monday afternoon game. The scorer of the Black Cats' goal remains a mystery and is the only officially unattributed goal in Sunderland's first team history, although some sources gave it to Jimmy Hannah.

Billy Hughes

SEPTEMBER 8

2003 Death of 1950s Scottish international left back Joe McDonald aged 74 in Adelaide.

2001 Niall Quinn scored the only goal against Blackburn Rovers to give Sunderland their second successive 1-0 home win. This was Scottish midfielder Alex Rae's final game for The Lads.

1979 First half goals from Mick Buckley and Shaun Elliott gave Sunderland a 2-0 win over Cambridge United.

1934 A Patsy Gallacher hat trick helped Sunderland beat Chelsea 4-0 to maintain top spot in Division One.

SEPTEMBER 9

2006 Chris Brown and Ross Wallace turned a half time deficit into a 2-1 win at Derby County in Roy Keane's first game in charge.

1989 Marco Gabbiadini tormented his marker, future Magpies' boss Glenn Roeder, scoring a hat trick as Watford were beaten 4-0 at Roker Park to move Sunderland into second place in Division Two. The third goal made him the first Sunderland player to score fifty goals for ten years.

1975 Tony Towers became the first Sunderland player to be sent off in the League Cup when he was dismissed at Notts County in a second round tie.

1962 Scottish international outside left George Mulhall signed from Aberdeen for £25,000.

09.09.2006

Marco Gabbiadini

SEPTEMBER 10

2005 Sunderland's run of defeats from the start of the season extended to five as The Lads went down 2-0 at Premiership champions Chelsea. Justin Hoyte made his debut after being signed on a season long loan from Arsenal.

1966 Defender Colin Todd made his debut as a substitute for Charlie Hurley in a 1-1 draw at Chelsea.

1955 The Black Cats recover from being 3-1 down at half time to beat Chelsea 4-3 at Roker Park courtesy of a brace each from Charlie Fleming and Ken Chisholm.

1898 Roker Park staged its first League game; a 1-0 win over Liverpool with James Leslie getting the only goal. Hugh Wilson was the only player to have played in Sunderland's first League game and this first game at Roker Park.

SEPTEMBER 11

2007 Death of 1973 FA Cup final goalscoring hero Ian Porterfield aged 61.

2004 After winning only one of the first six League games, The Lads found their form with a 4-0 triumph at Gillingham. Marcus Stewart's hat trick was his first for Sunderland.

1935 Raich Carter scored four goals for the only time in his Sunderland career as The Lads thrashed West Bromwich Albion 6-1 at Roker Park.

1933 Birth of Ambrose Fogarty in Dublin who was the first League player to be sent off in all three major domestic competitions; FA Cup whilst with Sunderland; League and League Cup with Hartlepool United.

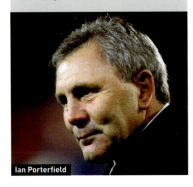

Ian Porterfield

SEPTEMBER 12

2001 Lilian Laslandes got his only goal for Sunderland and Michael Ingham made his debut in the League Cup second round 4-2 defeat at Hillsborough; played on the day after the Twin Towers in New York were subjected to a terrorist attack.

1953 Reigning League champions Arsenal suffered their worst defeat on Wearside when Sunderland beat them 7-1. Trevor Ford got a hat trick and Tommy Wright a brace with Billy Elliott and Len Shackleton completing the rout.

1925 David Halliday scored his second successive hat trick, and made it ten goals in his first four games for Sunderland, when The Lads beat Sheffield United 6-1 at Roker Park.

1914 Jackie Mordue scored Sunderland's quickest penalty; awarded after only thirty seconds of the home game against Liverpool.

SEPTEMBER 13

2006 Liam Miller, Graham Kavanagh and Stephen Elliott ensured Roy Keane's second game in charge also ended in a victory. Leeds United were comprehensively beaten 3-0 at Elland Road moving Sunderland seven places up the League.

2003 A coolly taken injury time penalty from Marcus Stewart secured a 2-1 home win over Crystal Palace extending the winning sequence to four games.

1913 Two second half goals from James Richardson helped defending League champions Sunderland to a 3-1 win at Liverpool.

1890 Sunderland played their first League game; against Burnley at Newcastle Road. John Spence scored Sunderland's first ever League goal in this 3-2 defeat in front of an estimated 5,000 crowd.

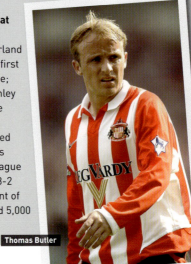

Thomas Butler

SEPTEMBER 14

2004 First half goals from Julio Arca and Stephen Wright gave Sunderland a 2-0 home victory over Nottingham Forest moving them up to 8th place in The Championship.

1999 Thomas Butler made his debut and Chris Lumsdon his final appearance in Sunderland's 3-2 League Cup second round first leg win at home to Walsall.

1944 Long serving right back Jack Stelling signed from Usworth Grange. Sunderland proved to be his only League club during his fourteen year career.

1926 Forward Frank Cresswell made his debut in a goalless draw at Huddersfield Town with his brother, Warney, appearing at right back. This made them the first brothers to play in a League game for Sunderland.

SEPTEMBER 15

1998 Sunderland set themselves up for a comfortable passage through to the next round of the League Cup with a 3-0 home win over Chester City in the first leg of the second round.

1958 Birth of goalkeeper Chris Turner in Sheffield.

1954 Centre half Fred Hall made his final appearance for the Black Cats in a goalless home draw with Wolves.

1890 Long serving keeper William Kirkley was blamed for letting a 3-0 half time lead slip as Sunderland lost their second ever League game 4-3; at home to Wolverhampton Wanderers. Even though Kirkley was reckoned to be ill this proved to be his final game for Sunderland. (see September 20th)

SEPTEMBER 16

2006 Trinidad & Tobago international Dwight Yorke made his debut as a substitute in Roy Keane's first home game in charge; a 1-1 draw with Leicester City. The crowd of 35,104 was an increase of almost 11,000 on the previous home game.

2000 Goals from two Kevins, Kilbane and Phillips, gave The Lads a 2-1 win over Derby County and maintained their unbeaten home start to the season.

1986 Central defender Nigel Saddington became the first Sunderland debutant to play 120 minutes. The Full Members' Cup tie against Barnsley went to extra-time and then was settled 8-7 on penalties. He also became the first debutant to take and score a penalty in a shoot out.

1922 Sunderland's most prolific League goal scorer Charlie Buchan netted four times in a 5-1 victory over Bolton Wanderers at Roker Park.

Chris Turner
16.09.2000

SEPTEMBER 17

2005 An injury time goal from West Brom's Zoltan Gera denied Sunderland their first victory of the season. However the 1-1 draw did give them their first point back in the Premiership after five successive defeats.

1991 Striker Marco Gabbiadini scored his last goals for Sunderland, a six minute second half hat trick in a 4-1 victory over Charlton Athletic at their temporary Upton Park home.

1981 Central defender Sam Allardyce transferred to Millwall for £75,000 after only one season on Wearside.

1890 Scottish international goalkeeper Teddy Doig signed from Arbroath to replace William Kirkley. (see September 20th)

SEPTEMBER 18

2004 Darren Carter, on loan from Birmingham City, scored just before half time on his debut as Sunderland beat Preston North End 3-1 at the Stadium of Light.

1999 The Black Cats recorded their best top flight away victory for more than 52 years as Derby County were trounced 5-0 thanks to a Kevin Phillips hat trick and goals from Gavin McCann and Niall Quinn.

1917 Billy Cringan transferred to Celtic for £600. Sunderland needed this money to stay in business following the loss in revenue caused by WW1.

(see May 19th)

1912 Goalkeeper Walter Scott let in four goals at home to Blackburn making it ten conceded in three games. It was his last game as he was sacked for missing training the following day when he went to visit his mother.

SEPTEMBER 19

1998 The Black Cats started their home game against Oxford United without the usual strike force of Phillips and Quinn. However this did not prevent the avalanche of goals that followed as Oxford conceded seven without reply. Bridges, Dichio and Rae each got a brace as well as one from Michael Gray.

1973 Sunderland played their first game in one of the major European Cup tournaments; a first round first leg European Cup Winners' Cup tie in Hungary against Vasas Budapest. Billy Hughes scored The Lads' first goal in a 2-0 victory which also marked the last occasion that the 1973 FA Cup winning team played together.

1941 Birth of Northern Irish international defender Martin Harvey in Belfast.

1891 Hugh Wilson became the first Sunderland player to score from a penalty; at Bolton Wanderers. The Football League had only introduced this rule for an infringement in the penalty area during that summer.

(see November 21st)

SEPTEMBER 20

2004 Death of legendary goal scorer for Sunderland and Middlesbrough, and later successful manager, Brian Clough aged 69.

2003 Estonian Mart Poom became the first Sunderland goalkeeper to score in a competitive game when he rose imperiously to head in a 92nd minute Sean Thornton corner against his former club, Derby County. This gave The Lads a 1-1 draw at Pride Park.

1958 Cec Irwin, Len Ashurst and Jimmy McNab all made their debuts in the home game against Ipswich Town. Between them they went on to appear more than 1100 times for The Lads.

1890 Teddy Doig made his debut at West Bromwich Albion in a 4-0 win. However Sunderland were deducted the two points and fined £50 as Doig had not completed the necessary fourteen day registration period and was therefore ineligible to play.

(see September 17th)

20.09.2003

SEPTEMBER 21

2004 Debutant Chris Brown scored twice as Sunderland drew 3-3 after extra time at Crewe Alexandra in a second round League Cup tie. However The Lads went out of the competition losing the subsequent penalty shoot out 4-2.

1999 Marcos Di Giuseppe, known as Bica, became the first Brazilian to play for Sunderland. His 45 minute second half appearance in a 5-0 second round second leg League Cup victory at Walsall was his only one for the club.

1935 Patsy Gallacher struck a hat trick and Bobby Gurney a brace in Sunderland's 7-2 home victory over Blackburn Rovers.

1930 Birth of Bob Stokoe, christened "The Messiah" after steering Sunderland to victory in the 1973 FA Cup final less than six months after becoming their manager.

SEPTEMBER 22

2001 A brace from Niall Quinn gave Sunderland a 2-2 draw at home to Charlton Athletic having been 1-0 down at half time.

1987 Striker Marco Gabbiadini was signed from York City by his former boss Denis Smith for £80,000. He became an instant hero by scoring six goals in his first four games.

1891 Birth of record League goalscorer and 1920s captain Charlie Buchan in Plumpstead, London.

1888 Sunderland played their first game against an international team. They lost 3-0 to a Canadian Tourists team at Newcastle Road.

Marco Gabbiadini

SEPTEMBER 23

1997 The 2-1 victory at Bury in a League Cup second round second leg match marked the final appearances of Steve Agnew and Paul Bracewell. It was also goalkeeper Edwin Zoetebier's debut.

1978 Sunderland won 2-1 at Turf Moor thanks to two Gary Rowell goals. This is the only time that the Black Cats have won a game having been reduced to nine men; full backs Mick Henderson and Joe Bolton had been sent off just before half time with the game still goalless.

1961 A 4-0 home win over Scunthorpe United, thanks to twin strikes from Herd and Fogarty, started a run of only one defeat in seventeen games that took Sunderland from 19th up to 3rd in Division Two.

1919 Birth of half back Arthur Wright in Burradon, Northumberland. His 281 appearances in an 18 year spell at Sunderland showed how his career was impacted by the lack of first team football during WW2.

SEPTEMBER 24

2004 Sunderland gained their second successive 1-0 away win at Elland Road thanks to a second half strike by Welsh international Carl Robinson.

1962 Birth of Scottish international striker Ally McCoist in Bellshill, Glasgow. On the same day Sunderland recorded their highest home victory in the League Cup; 7-1 against Oldham Athletic.

1946 Birth of 1960s forward John O'Hare in Renton.

1892 A brace from Johnny Campbell took his goal tally to eight in the opening four games of the season as Sunderland comfortably beat Blackburn Rovers 5-0 at Newcastle Road.

24.09.2004

SEPTEMBER 25

2005 A second minute Tommy Miller strike and a second half Julio Arca free kick gave Sunderland their first win of the season; 2-0 at Middlesbrough.

1982 Sunderland equalled their worst ever League defeat going down 8-0 at Watford.

1971 Jimmy Hamilton became Sunderland's youngest outfield player when he came on as a substitute for Brian Chambers aged 16 years 103 days. He scored after being on the field for only five minutes thus becoming the youngest scorer as well.

1961 Roker Park staged its first League Cup tie; a first round replay against Bolton Wanderers that Sunderland won 1-0.

SEPTEMBER 26

1991 Striker Marco Gabbiadini transferred to Crystal Palace with Sunderland receiving a then record fee of £1.8 million.

1987 Sunderland sat 12th in Division Three, the lowest position in their history, following a 2-0 home defeat to Chester City. However the game, Marco Gabbiadini's debut, marked a turning point as six successive wins followed taking The Lads to the top of the division.

1957 "King" Charlie Hurley signed from Millwall for £18,000.

1908 The referee in the Sunderland v Nottingham Forest game blew for half time after only 43 minutes. He realised his error during half time and the players came out and played two minutes kicking in the original direction before he called half time again. At which point the players changed ends for the second half.

SEPTEMBER 27

2003 Striker Tommy Smith made his debut as a substitute for Thomas Butler in a 2-0 home victory over Reading.

1980 Gary Rowell scored his first League goal for 18 months as Sunderland beat Leeds United 4-1 at Roker Park. He had struggled to regain his form following a serious knee injury towards the end of the 1978-79 season.

1961 Brian Clough scored his first hat trick for Sunderland in a 3-0 home win over Bury. This took his goals tally to nine in eleven games after signing from Middlesbrough.

1924 Charlie Buchan scored the first goal in a 2-1 win at Bolton Wanderers. In doing so he became the first Sunderland player to score 200 League goals; achieved in his 347th League game for The Lads.

SEPTEMBER 28

2002 Sunderland recorded their first home win of the season thanks to a second half goal from David Bellion against Aston Villa.

1996 Martin Scott and Paul Stewart were sent off in the first half at Highbury. Peter Reid was also sent to the stands for protesting against Stewart's dismissal; a second yellow card for handball. The Lads defended staunchly but eventually succumbed 2-0.

1963 Right half and former Sunderland captain Stan Anderson played his 447th, and final, game for Sunderland in a 3-3 home draw against Cardiff City. This was a record for an outfield player until passed by Len Ashurst. (see March 21st)

1916 Birth of long serving outside right Len Duns in Newcastle. One of the many players whose career was severely curtailed by WW2.

SEPTEMBER 29

2000 Defender Darren Holloway became the first player to be transferred to Wimbledon. The fee was £1.25 million.

1971 Kerr, Watson, Tueart and Hughes all hit the target in a 4-1 home victory over Middlesbrough.

1939 Birth of Scottish international "Slim Jim" Baxter in Hill of Beath, Fife.

1894 Prolific Victorian centre forward Johnny Campbell scored his 100th League goal in his 102nd League game; a 4-1 defeat at Bolton Wanderers. This remains the quickest that any Sunderland player has achieved this feat.

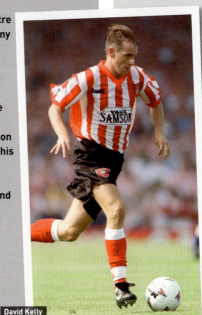

David Kelly

SEPTEMBER 30

2006 Grant Leadbitter gave Roy Keane his first home win with a second half strike against Sheffield Wednesday.

1995 Republic of Ireland striker David Kelly scored on his home debut, along with Andy Melville, in a 2-2 draw with Reading.

1972 A 4-1 home victory over Nottingham Forest included a brace from John Lathan in what proved to be Alan Brown's 200th, and final, victory as Sunderland manager during his two spells with the Black Cats.

1950 Ivor Broadis scored the first of his two Sunderland hat tricks in a 4-2 home win over Charlton Athletic.

OCTOBER

OCTOBER 1

2002 Sunderland thrashed Cambridge United 7-0 at the Abbey Stadium to record their biggest winning margin in the League Cup and also their best away win since the 9-1 victory at Newcastle United. (see December 5th)

1994 Alec Chamberlain became Sunderland's first goalkeeping substitute in a League game when he replaced the injured Tony Norman at home to Southend United. (see August 11th)

1983 A first half Gary Rowell penalty gave Sunderland all of the points at Anfield.

1923 Birth of Welsh international centre forward Trevor Ford in Swansea. (see November 4th)

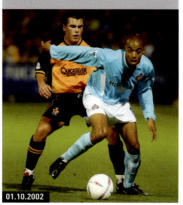

01.10.2002

OCTOBER 2

1999 Sunderland achieved their highest position in the Premiership, second place, after a 4-0 away win against Bradford City. Kevin Phillips' two goals took him to ten in ten League games.

1982 All of the goals came in the second half as Sunderland beat Norwich City 4-1 at Roker Park. Ally McCoist netted one of these and started a run of five goals in six games for The Lads.

1926 Goals from Marshall (2), Coglin and Ellis sealed a 4-1 home victory over Sheffield Wednesday taking Sunderland to the top of Division One.

1922 Birth of diminutive post WW2 outside left Tommy Reynolds in Felling.

OCTOBER 3

1984 Sunderland had three players sent off in a game for the first, and so far only, time. Barry Venison, Paul Lemon and Clive Walker were all dismissed during a "friendly" at Hammarby in Sweden.

1979 Debutant John Hawley set up 'Pop' Robson's winner in Sunderland's 1-0 League Cup third round replay victory over First Division Manchester City at Roker Park.

1973 Roker Park staged its first European Cup Winners' Cup tie. Dennis Tueart scored from the spot in the 1-0 first round second leg game against Vasas Budapest. (see September 19th)

1948 Birth of 1973 FA Cup winning centre forward Vic Halom in Coton Park near Burton-upon-Trent.

OCTOBER 4

2003 A diving header from Kevin Kyle was enough to take all the points at Bramall Lane despite The Lads being reduced to ten men following the dismissal of Julio Arca.

1961 Jim Montgomery made his debut in a 5-2 home victory over Walsall in a second round League Cup tie. Brian Clough's hat trick in this game was the first by a Sunderland player in this competition.

1936 Birth of Eire international defender and fan's Player of the Century, Charlie Hurley, in Cork.

1912 Goalkeeper Joe Butler signed from Glossop North End for £3,000. Following his signing, Sunderland, with two points from the opening six games, rose from near the foot of the First Division to being crowned Champions and FA Cup runners up the following April.

OCTOBER 5

1991 Irish defender Anton Rogan made his debut at home to Brighton & Hove Albion. The Lads recovered from a 2-1 half time deficit to win 4-2. Sunderland's first goal was Peter Beagrie's only strike during his month long loan from Everton.

1974 Two second half goals from `Pop' Robson sealed a 2-0 home victory over Oxford United and kept Sunderland second in the Second Division.

1957 Charlie Hurley made his debut at centre half in a 7-0 defeat at Blackpool. His second game a week later, at Burnley, was only marginally better as The Lads lost 6-0.

1946 Birth of England centre half Dave Watson in Stapleford, Nottinghamshire.

Charlie Hurley

OCTOBER 6

1979 Centre forward John Hawley scored a hat trick on his League debut in the 4-0 home victory over Charlton Athletic.

1976 Record appearance holder Jim Montgomery made his 627th, and final, first team appearance for Sunderland in a League Cup third round second replay at Manchester United.

1966 Birth of former player, Eire international, manager and current chairman Niall Quinn in Dublin.

1926 Sunderland remained at the head of the top flight with a 7-1 home victory over Burnley thanks to hat tricks from David Halliday and Stephen Coglin.

OCTOBER 7

2002 Peter Reid's almost 7 year reign as Sunderland manager ended when he was sacked by chairman Bob Murray.

1995 Sunderland took all three points at Crystal Palace, despite missing two penalties, thanks to a second half David Kelly goal.

1911 Outside right Robert Best scored on his debut in a 3-1 home victory over Aston Villa as The Lads came back from 1-0 down at half time.

1899 Sunderland's one and only visit to Glossop North End for a League game ended in a 2-0 victory thanks to goals from Colin McLatchie and Thomas Becton.

Peter Reid

OCTOBER 8

1994 A goal from Martin Smith and a double from Phil Gray gave the Black Cats a 3-1 victory at West Bromwich Albion.

1972 Birth of central defender Stanislav Varga in Lippany; the first Slovak to play for Sunderland.

1966 Striker Nick Sharkey made his final appearance, his 99th League start, in a 2-2 home draw with West Bromwich Albion.

1912 Sunderland signed right back Charlie Gladwin from Blackpool for £1,000. The Lads won 26 out of 36 games he played in during the remainder of the season claiming both their fifth top flight Championship and FA Cup runners up spot.

Jim Montgomery

OCTOBER 9

1994 Death of 1930s legend, and only Sunderland born player to lift the FA Cup, Raich Carter aged 80.

1990 Sunderland won 6-1 at Bristol City to record their best ever away win in the League Cup. This second round second leg result has since been bettered at Cambridge United. (see October 1st)

1954 Roker Park's second highest League crowd of 66,654 watched Sunderland beat Newcastle United 4-2 to go top of Division One. The goals came from Purdon, Bingham (2) and Chisholm. (see March 4th)

1943 Birth of Jimmy Montgomery in Sunderland; long remembered for his incredible double save in the 1973 FA Cup Final.

OCTOBER 10

2002 Howard Wilkinson and Steve Cotterill appointed as manager and assistant manager of Sunderland.

1999 Striker Kevin Phillips became the first Sunderland player to appear for England at the Stadium of Light in a 2-1 friendly victory over Belgium.

1987 Sunderland's `G force' helped The Lads to a 4-1 home win over Wigan Athletic putting them top of Division Three. Eric Gates and Marco Gabbiadini both scored twice in the game.

1925 Sunderland beat Everton 7-3 at Roker Park in a game that included two strikes each from Bobby Marshall and David Halliday. This meant The Lads had scored 25 goals in the first five home games of the season.

OCTOBER 11

1980 Birth of defender Nyron Nosworthy in Brixton, London.

1975 A Tony Towers penalty and goals from Billy Hughes and `Pop' Robson sealed a 3-1 home victory over Orient keeping Sunderland top of Division Two.

1967 Sunderland won 3-2 at Everton in a League Cup third round tie in front of a 39,914 crowd.

1882 Birth of Arthur Bridgett in Forsbrook, Stoke. He refused to play on religious days as he was an active member of The Brotherhood Movement.

10.10.1999

OCTOBER 12

1985 Peter Daniel made his final Sunderland appearance in a 1-1 home draw against one of his former clubs, Hull City. The draw left the Black Cats next to bottom of Division Two.

1968 Right back Cec Irwin scored his only goal for Sunderland, in over 350 appearances, in a 3-1 home victory over Nottingham Forest.

1912 Sunderland won their first game of their title winning season at the eighth attempt. The 4-0 home victory over Middlesbrough sparked a run of twelve wins in fifteen games.

1907 Sunderland outside right James Raine was in the Football League XI that beat an Irish League XI 6-3 at Roker Park.

Cec Irwin

OCTOBER 13

2001 A second half Kevin Phillips goal in front of a new record crowd, 48,305, at the Stadium of Light proved only a consolation as Manchester United won 3-1. (see April 13th)

1976 Striker Bryan `Pop' Robson was sold back to his former club West Ham United for £80,000. He was to rejoin and leave Sunderland on two more occasions in his career that included three spells on Wearside.

1970 Right back Dick Malone signed from Ayr United for £30,000.

1907 Birth of Sunderland's record goal scorer Bobby Gurney in Silksworth.

OCTOBER 14

2000 A Kevin Phillips penalty gave Sunderland all the points at home to Chelsea in a game delayed by 45 minutes due to a power failure.

1989 The Gabbiadini brothers never played first team football together at Sunderland. The nearest occasion was when Ricardo made his only first team appearance coming on as substitute for his elder brother, Marco, in a 2-0 defeat at Leeds United.

1933 A Patsy Gallacher hat trick and a goal from Benny Yorston on his 28th birthday gave Sunderland a 4-1 home win over Liverpool.

1896 Centre half John Auld became the first player to be transferred to Newcastle United. He received £20 for turning professional and £150 signing on fee.

OCTOBER 15

1996 Middlesbrough born Darren Williams signed from York City for £50,000 plus appearance based payments.

1977 Second half goals from Kevin Arnott and Gary Rowell gave Sunderland a 2-0 home win over Millwall. This was their first win for almost two months.

1955 Death of pre-WW1 right back William Troughear aged 70. His surname prompted the nickname "Tough Lugs".

1932 Debut of inside forward Raich Carter in a 3-1 defeat at Hillsbrough.

William 'Tough Lugs' Troughear

OCTOBER 16

2004 Sunderland's home game with Millwall was settled by a second half own goal from Kevin Muscat.

1976 Bob Stokoe stood down as Sunderland manager due to ill health following a 1-0 home defeat by Aston Villa. Assistant manager Ian McFarlane took over in a caretaker role for the next seven games. (see November 30th)

1965 Martin Harvey took over in goal for the injured Montgomery with seven minutes of the game remaining. The score remained the same as Sunderland came out 3-2 victors at home to Nottingham Forest.

1909 England international George Holley scored a hat trick in Sunderland's 6-2 home victory over Arsenal.

OCTOBER 17

1987 Sunderland won at Blackpool 2-0 thanks to a brace from central defender John MacPhail.

1966 Centre half George Kinnell, cousin of Jim Baxter, signed from Oldham Athletic for £20,000.

1936 Middlesbrough and Sunderland drew 5-5 at Ayresome Park. This equalled their highest ever scoring draw. (see January 19th)

1879 On this Friday night Scottish teacher James Allan is thought to have met with other teachers at the British Day School in Norfolk Street, Hendon. The outcome of this meeting was the formation of Sunderland & District Teachers' Association Football Club; later to become SAFC.

George Kinnell

OCTOBER 18

1999 Sunderland came back from a goal down on Sky TV to beat Aston Villa 2-1 thanks to a penalty then a late header from Kevin Phillips. This was their fifth successive top flight win; their best run at this level since 1936.

1998 A dramatic second half comeback saw the Black Cats turn a 2-0 half time deficit at The Hawthorns into a 3-2 victory. Captain Kevin Ball netted the winner four minutes from the end.

1961 A Football Association XI lost 2-1 to an Army team at Roker Park. Private James Baxter of Glasgow Rangers, and later Sunderland, was in the forces doing National Service and starred for the Army side.

1924 Roker Park witnessed its first crowd in excess of fifty thousand; 55,642 watched the 1-1 draw against Newcastle United.

OCTOBER 19

2002 Howard Wilkinson's first game in charge coincided with Niall Quinn's final appearance for The Lads. Neither enjoyed the result as Sunderland lost 1-0 at home to West Ham United.

1996 Goalkeeper Tony Coton suffered a double fracture of his right leg at Southampton. Lionel Perez came on as a substitute keeper to make his debut. This proved to be Coton's final appearance for Sunderland.

1991 The Black Cats staged a remarkable recovery at Port Vale to salvage a point after trailing 3-0 with only 34 minutes left. Goals from Kevin Ball and Kieron Brady (2) levelled matters and they could even have stolen all three points had Brady converted a golden chance late on to complete his hat trick.

1968 England World Cup hero Geoff Hurst scored six times as West Ham United inflicted a record equalling defeat on Sunderland. The Hammers scored four times in each half without reply. (see September 25th and December 26th)

OCTOBER 20

2003 Sunderland Reserves became the first team from the Club to settle a game by a golden goal; Jack Wanless scored after 100 minutes to beat Whickham 1-0 in the Durham Challenge Cup.

1979 First half goals from Robson (2) and Hawley gave Sunderland all of the points at home to Queens Park Rangers who had taken to the field in Sunderland's blue away shirts.

1940 Birth of Neil Martin in Selston, Nottinghamshire; the last Sunderland player before Kevin Phillips to score twenty top flight goals in a season (1966-67).

1926 Albert McInroy became the first, and so far last, Sunderland goalkeeper to be capped by England in a full international. He was between the sticks, along with colleague Warney Cresswell at right back, against Ireland at Anfield in a 3-3 draw.

OCTOBER 21

2006 Veteran Irish defender Kenny Cunningham made the final appearance of his brief Wearside career in a 2-0 home win against Barnsley.

1978 A brace from Gary Rowell and one from Alan Brown gave Sunderland a 3-2 home win over Millwall.

1940 Birth of 1960s full back and midfielder Calvin Palmer in Skegness.

1911 A brace from George Holley, his second in successive away games, gave The Lads a 2-0 victory at Sheffield United.

Calvin Palmer

OCTOBER 22

1988 Two goals in each half gave Sunderland a 4-0 home victory over Swindon Town.

1983 Sunderland's shirts carried a sponsor's logo for the first time, Cowies, for the home game against Manchester United. This game was scheduled to be on BBC TV's Match of the Day but an industrial dispute caused the programme to be cancelled.

1955 The Black Cats went top of Division One with a 3-2 win at Spurs. By this stage Sunderland had netted 35 goals in the first twelve games of the season.

1904 Billy Hogg became the first Sunderland player to be sent off in a home game. He was dismissed shortly after giving Sunderland a 3-0 lead against Sheffield Wednesday.

OCTOBER 23

1991 Republic of Ireland striker John Byrne joined Sunderland from Brighton & Hove Albion for £225,000.

1962 Northern Irish international forward John Crossan was signed from Belgian side Standard Liege for £26,700.

1920 Sunderland drew 2-2 at Bradford City with Charlie Parker, Jack Mitton and Bobby Marshall making their debuts. Seventeen and a half year old Marshall netted on his debut to become Sunderland's youngest scorer.
(see September 25th)

1897 The Newcastle Road ground had its largest attendance, estimated at 22,000, for a goalless draw with Aston Villa.

OCTOBER 24

1998 A Danny Dichio goal gave Sunderland a 1-0 home victory over Bury taking them back to the top of Division One. They stayed in this position for the remainder of the season thus clinching promotion back to the Premiership.

1978 Birth of winger Carlos Edwards in Diego Martin, Trinidad.

1973 Sunderland beat Sporting Lisbon 2-1 at Roker Park in the European Cup Winners' Cup second round first leg.

1947 Prolific WW2 scorer Cliff Whitelum transferred to Sheffield United for £9,000.

John Crossan

25.10.2008

OCTOBER 25

2008 A Djibril Cisse goal and a thunderbolt free kick from Kieran Richardson gave Sunderland their first home win over Newcastle United for 28 years.

1978 Manager Jimmy Adamson resigned to join Leeds United with assistant Dave Merrington stepping up to take charge in a caretaker capacity.

1930 Jarrow born keeper Jimmy Thorpe made his debut and Tommy Urwin scored a hat trick in Sunderland's 4-2 victory over Huddersfield Town; their first home win of the season.

1890 Johnny Campbell scored the first League hat trick for Sunderland in a 5-2 win at Bolton Wanderers. In fact he scored four times as The Lads came back from a 2-1 half time deficit in their seventh ever League game.

OCTOBER 26

1993 Sunderland threw everything at Aston Villa yet ended up 4-1 losers thanks to brilliant keeping by Mark Bosnich. Villa went on to lift the League Cup after surviving this difficult third round tie at Roker Park.

1960 The newly created League Cup saw Sunderland drawn at Brentford for their first ever tie. Although The Lads led 3-1 at half time thanks to goals from Lawther, McPheat and Fogarty the Londoners came out 4-3 winners.

1946 Sunderland beat Manchester United 3-0, thanks to a Cliff Whitelum hat trick, at Maine Road. United were using City's ground for home games because Old Trafford was closed due to bomb damage.

1929 Centre forward David Halliday transferred to Arsenal for £6,500 after scoring 162 goals in only 175 first team appearances for Sunderland.

OCTOBER 27

2001 Sunderland drew 1-1 at home to Arsenal thanks to a Stefan Schwarz goal. However they thought they had grabbed a dramatic injury time winner only to see Julio Arca's header ruled out for offside.

1965 A crowd of 31,828 turned out for Brian Clough's testimonial at Roker Park against a Newcastle United Select XI.

1950 Welsh international centre forward Trevor Ford was signed from Aston Villa for a British record fee of £29,500.

1888 Centre forward John Breconridge scored Sunderland's first hat trick in the FA Cup; in a 5-3 home victory over Elswick Rangers.

Stefan Schwarz

OCTOBER 28

2006 A last minute strike by Ross Wallace gave Sunderland a 1-0 win at Hull City. However he received a second yellow card for his goal celebrations and was therefore sent off.

2002 USA captain Claudio Reyna ruptured a knee ligament in a 1-1 draw at Bolton Wanderers which kept him out for the rest of the season. This proved to be his last game for Sunderland.

1961 Brian Clough scored his third home hat trick in a month as Plymouth Argyle were defeated 5-0. This meant he had scored twelve goals in the last five home games.

1936 Sunderland beat Arsenal 2-1 at Roker Park in their first ever Charity Shield game courtesy of second half goals from Burbanks and Carter.

OCTOBER 29

1966 Sunderland recorded a 3-0 win at St James' Park, their best for 58 years, thanks to goals from Mulhall, Martin and O'Hare. (see December 5th)

1932 Sunderland beat Bolton Wanderers 7-4 at Roker Park having been 6-2 up at half time. Bobby Gurney scored four with Connor, Carter and Temple getting the rest.

1898 Hugh Wilson scored the first hat trick by a Sunderland player at Roker Park in the 3-0 victory over Bury.

1866 Birth of goalkeeper John Edward Doig in Letham, Forfarshire; holder of a record four top flight Championship medals (shared with Jimmy Millar) whilst with Sunderland.

OCTOBER 30

2004 Second half goals from Julio Arca and Liam Lawrence (penalty) were sufficient to see off Brighton 2-0 at the Stadium of Light.

1976 Sunderland ended a period of 6 years 209 days without a top flight victory, the longest in their history, when they won 2-1 at Coventry City. Bob Lee, with his first for the club, and Billy Hughes got the goals.

1954 Ken Chisholm, Billy Bingham and Stan Anderson (penalty) gave Sunderland a 3-1 victory at Highbury in front of 65,423 people; their third match in front of a crowd in excess of sixty thousand that month.

1909 George Holley scored his second successive home hat trick as Sunderland beat Chelsea 4-0.

OCTOBER 31

2000 Don Hutchison scored twice in Sunderland's 2-1 League Cup third round win at Bristol Rovers. This was Paul Butler's and Michael Reddy's final game for The Lads.

1999 Two first half goals by Niall Quinn gave Sunderland a 2-1 win over Tottenham Hotspur keeping them in third place in the Premiership.

1973 Vic Halom scored his only hat trick for the Club as Sunderland finally overcame Derby County 3-0 in a League Cup second round second replay at Roker Park.

1908 English internationals Arthur Brown, George Holley and Arthur Bridgett scored two goals each as Sunderland beat Manchester United 6-1 at Roker Park.

Don Hutchison

NOVEMBER

NOVEMBER 1

2003 Debut of winger Stewart Downing in a goalless draw at The Hawthorns. This was the start of a seven game loan spell from Middlesbrough in which he scored three times.

1998 Johnston, Quinn and Bridges scored as Sunderland comfortably beat Colin Todd's Bolton Wanderers at the Reebok Stadium in a Sunday afternoon televised game.

1972 Alan Brown was sacked thus ending his second spell in charge of Sunderland. Coach and former player Billy Elliott stepped up into the caretaker manager role until Bob Stokoe was appointed. (see November 29th)

1952 Welsh centre forward Trevor Ford scored four goals, including a penalty, in Sunderland's 5-2 victory at Manchester City.

Alan Brown

NOVEMBER 2

1991 Jarrow born Craig Russell made his debut coming on as a substitute for David Rush in a 3-1 home victory over Watford.

1963 A brace from John Crossan and one from George Herd gave The Lads a 3-0 home victory over Grimsby Town moving them up to top spot in Division Two.

1935 Debut of outside right Len Duns in a 2-2 draw at Portsmouth. This proved to be the start of a sixteen year career with his only League club in which he won a League Championship and FA Cup winners medal before he had turned 21.

1928 Birth of 1950s Welsh international centre half Ray Daniel in Swansea.

NOVEMBER 3

1992 Goals from Cunnington and Goodman gave Sunderland a rare home victory; 2-0 over Wolves, in a season long struggle to avoid relegation.

1987 Both Richard Ord and Michael Heathcote made their debuts, and Eric Gates scored four times, in a 7-0 home rout over Southend United. This was Sunderland's highest victory for 31 years. (see September 1st)

1962 Grimsby Town were heavily defeated, 6-2, at Roker Park with Brian Clough scoring what turned out to be his seventh, and final, hat trick for Sunderland.

1937 Seaham born outside left Fred Rowell played his only first team game in a 2-0 Charity Shield defeat at Manchester City.

NOVEMBER 4

2003 Sunderland won 3-1 at Gillingham thanks to goals from Downing, his first for the Club, Oster and Stewart.

1954 England football and cricket international Willie Watson left Sunderland to become player manager of Halifax Town.

1950 Centre forward Trevor Ford had an eventful home debut against Sheffield Wednesday. He scored a hat trick in a 5-1 win, accidentally broke the opposing centre half's jaw and split a goal post when he and the Wednesday keeper collided with it.

1893 Wolverhampton Wanderers were comprehensively beaten 6-0 at Newcastle Road with Jimmy Millar netting one of his ten hat tricks for the Club.

Willie Watson

NOVEMBER 5

1983 The Black Cats extended their unbeaten run at Highbury to five games, and spoiled future Arsenal captain Tony Adams' debut, with a 2-1 victory courtesy of goals from Colin West and Ian Atkins.

1966 Sunderland converted a 3-0 half time score into a 4-1 home win over Sheffield United to extend their winning run in the top flight to three games.

1938 Stoke City were defeated 3-0 at Roker Park in a game that included Patsy Gallacher's last two goals for the Club taking his League total to exactly one hundred.

1887 Sunderland were drawn at home in the FA Cup for the first time. The game against Newcastle West End went to extra time with Sunderland coming out victors 3-1.

NOVEMBER 6

2002 Death of Sunderland's youngest ever captain Rob Hindmarch in Canada from motor neurone disease aged 41. Later that day the Black Cats came back from 2-0 down at half time to beat Arsenal 3-2 at Highbury in a League Cup third round tie.

1999 Number 31 Michael Reddy tapped in the rebound from Kevin Phillips' saved penalty at Middlesbrough to give The Lads a 1-1 draw. He became the first Sunderland player to score wearing a shirt with a squad number higher than 30.

1984 Howard Gayle scored in extra time to beat Nottingham Forest 1-0 and send Sunderland through to the fourth round of the League Cup.

1963 After almost 450 games for Sunderland Stan Anderson was transferred to Newcastle United for £19,000.

Rob Hindmarch

NOVEMBER 7

1998 The Black Cats continued their unbeaten start to the season with a 3-1 home victory over Grimsby Town.

1979 Sunderland lost 2-0 in their Centenary game against an England XI at Roker Park. Everton striker Bob Latchford scored both of the England goals.

1973 Sunderland's participation in the European Cup Winners' Cup ended with a 2-0 defeat, 3-2 on aggregate, in the second round second leg at Sporting Lisbon in front of 50,000 spectators.

1919 Death of "Team of all The Talents" Scottish goalkeeper Teddy Doig from Spanish flu aged 53.

NOVEMBER 8

1988 Marco Gabbiadini scored the only goal in Sunderland's first ever Simod Cup tie. The away match, against Charlton Athletic, was played in front of their lowest ever first team attendance and Sunderland's lowest post WW2 away crowd. Only 1,666 people turned up for this Tuesday night game.

1930 Half back Billy Clunas, nicknamed "The Penalty King" played his final game for the Black Cats; a 3-2 home win over Grimsby Town. He is Sunderland's record penalty scorer with at least 30 successful spot kicks during his seven year career on Wearside.

1929 Record goalscorer in one season David Halliday was transferred early in the following season to Arsenal for £6,500. (see April 27th)

1884 Sunderland played their first ever FA Cup tie losing 3-1 at Redcar with Don McColl getting the consolation goal in the second half.

NOVEMBER 9

1985 A brace from centre forward David Swindlehurst gave Sunderland a 2-1 home win in their first ever game against Wimbledon.

1956 Inside forward, and later Leeds United manager, Don Revie signed from Manchester City for £24,000.

1946 Cliff Whitelum, Len Duns and Jackie Robinson scored in a 3-0 win on Sunderland's first League visit to Ayresome Park following WW2.

1935 Preston North End were beaten 4-2 at Roker Park putting Sunderland top of Division One. They remained there for the rest of the season and claimed their sixth, and so far last, top flight Championship. (see April 13th)

NOVEMBER 10

2002 Niall Quinn announced his retirement due to a persistent back injury on the same day that second half goals from Phillips and Flo give The Lads a 2-0 home win over Spurs.

1976 Two goals from Bob Lee and one from Billy Hughes saw Sunderland come back from being 2-0 down at half time at Old Trafford to draw 3-3. The point moved them off the foot of the top flight table.

1973 Dennis Tueart completed his only hat trick for Sunderland in a 4-1 home win over Swindon.

1934 Goals from Patsy Gallacher and Bobby Gurney (2) gave Sunderland a 3-2 home win over Manchester City moving them up a place to the top of Division One.

NOVEMBER 11

1998 Premiership club Everton were beaten 5-4 on penalties at Goodison Park in a fourth round League Cup tie. Michael Bridges had given Sunderland a half time lead that was later equalised thus allowing goalkeeper Sorensen to be the hero by saving the last penalty.

1959 England beat France 2-0 in an U-23 international at Roker Park.

1945 Birth of striker and caretaker manager Bryan `Pop' Robson in Sunderland.

1922 Jock Paterson and Arthur "Tricky" Hawes scored second half goals as Sunderland beat The Magpies 2-0 at Roker Park.

Niall Quinn has to hang up his boots

NOVEMBER 12

1983 Midfielder Nigel Walker claimed the record of the shortest Sunderland career when he came on for the last eight minutes against Watford in a 3-0 home win. This proved to be his only first team appearance for The Lads. (see January 24th)

1980 Kevin Arnott and John Cooke scored second half goals as Manchester City were defeated 2-0 at Roker Park. This proved to be Argentinian Claudio Marangoni's final appearance for Sunderland.

1964 Birth of 1990s captain Kevin Ball in Hastings.

1931 Hendon born Horatio Stratton Carter fulfilled a boyhood dream when he signed professional forms with Sunderland.

Kevin Ball

NOVEMBER 13

2004 Steven Caldwell scored the only goal as Sunderland won on their first visit to Leicester City's Walkers Stadium.

1979 Lifelong Sunderland fan Stan Cummins was signed from Middlesbrough for a Club record fee of £300,000.

1937 Birth of Allan Hope in Leadgate who later became the only Sunderland player to change his name by deed poll whilst at the club; taking on his stepfather's surname O'Neill. He is also the only player to score for the club under two different surnames.

1880 Sunderland played their first ever competitive game; playing under their original name of Sunderland & District Teachers FC. They lost 1-0 at Ferryhill.

Nicky Summerbee

NOVEMBER 14

1997 Sunderland's Craig Russell and Manchester City's Nicky Summerbee swapped clubs.

1987 Sunderland played their first pre-Christmas FA Cup tie since 1888 as a result of being in the third tier of English football. Two Paul Atkinson goals against Darlington at Roker Park saw them progress through to the second round.

1964 George Hardwick was appointed Sunderland manager three and a half months after Alan Brown has resigned. During this period the Club's directors had selected the team for each game. His first decision was to make Brian Clough Youth Team manager. (see July 31st)

1891 The "Team of all The Talents" maintained their excellent home form with a 7-1 demolition of Derby County in which centre forward John Campbell scored four times. In total he scored 39 goals that season in 29 appearances.

NOVEMBER 15

1997 Sunderland won 4-1 at Portsmouth thanks to goals from Quinn, Clark, Johnston and Summerbee. This was the first time in 104 games that The Lads had won away from home after conceding the first goal (lost 90 and drawn 14).

1995 Ex-Sunderland captain Gary Bennett moved to Carlisle United on a free transfer after more than eleven years with the Club.

1950 England beat Wales 4-2 in the last full international to be played at Roker Park. Sunderland centre forward Trevor Ford scored both of the Welsh goals and Willie Watson played right half for England.

1947 Two goals each from Dickie Davis and Albert Quinn, his only goals for the Club, and one from Willie Watson gave Sunderland a 5-1 home victory over Liverpool.

NOVEMBER 16

1974 A brace from `Pop' Robson helped Sunderland to a 3-1 win against Fulham at Craven Cottage moving them up to second in the table.

1963 Sunderland's 4-1 home victory over Leyton Orient took them back to the top of Division Two. Outside right Tommy Mitchinson replaced Brian Usher in the first team change for eight games.

1947 Birth of Sunderland's 1973 FA Cup winning captain Bobby Kerr in Balloch.

1935 The Black Cats convincingly won 5-1 at Brentford thanks to goals from Gurney (2), Duns, Carter and Gallacher.

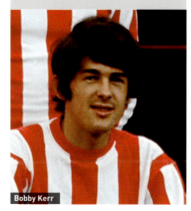
Bobby Kerr

NOVEMBER 17

2002 Sunderland extended their unbeaten run to five games with a goalless draw at Anfield. Sadly the improvement under new manager Howard Wilkinson was short lived and Sunderland were relegated at the end of the season.

1979 Stan Cummins scored on his debut in a 3-1 home win over Notts County.

1923 Charlie Buchan scored his fifth, and final, hat trick for The Lads in a 5-1 home win over Blackburn Rovers.

1888 Sunderland beat Newcastle East End 2-0 in a FA Cup third round qualifying game setting up the prospect of a local derby against rivals Sunderland Albion in the next round. (see December 8th)

NOVEMBER 18

2006 Colchester United were defeated 3-1 on their first ever visit to Wearside courtesy of a brace from Stephen Elliott and one from David Connolly, his first for the Club.

2000 Second half goals from Don Hutchison and Niall Quinn and an 85th minute penalty save by Thomas Sorensen from Alan Shearer gave Sunderland their second successive 2-1 victory at St James' Park.

1989 Sunderland moved up into fourth place in Division Two with a 3-1 home win over Plymouth Argyle. Kieron Brady made his debut coming on for Paul Hardyman.

1917 Birth of post WW2 centre half Fred Hall in the village of No Place, just outside Stanley, County Durham.

NOVEMBER 19

1966 Neil Martin, George Mulhall (2) and John O'Hare scored for Sunderland in their 4-3 home victory over Burnley.

1955 Top of the table, and Division One leading scorers, Sunderland were crushed 8-2 at twelfth placed Luton Town. South African Ted Purdon got both of the Black Cats' consolation goals.

1947 Birth of Sunderland's 1990 promotion winning team manager Denis Smith in Stoke.

1910 Goalkeeper Dick Roose broke his wrist in his 99th, and final appearance, for the Black Cats in a 1-1 draw at Newcastle United.

NOVEMBER 20

1999 Liverpool continued their unbeaten run on Wearside with a 2-0 win as The Lads suffered their first home defeat following their return to the Premiership. The gate of 42,015 set a new record for the Stadium of Light.

1976 Ray Train and Bob Lee scored in The Lads' 2-1 home victory over Spurs. These proved to be the last home League goals for almost three months as Sunderland went ten consecutive League games without scoring. (see February 11th)

1926 Sunderland went top of Division One with a 3-2 away win at Arsenal thanks to goals from Ellis, Halliday and Marshall.

1885 Birth of England international forward George Holley in Seaham Harbour.

NOVEMBER 21

1998 Sunderland's record unbeaten start to a season of 24 games came to an end with a 3-2 home defeat to Barnsley.

1992 Michael Gray made his debut as a substitute for Kevin Ball in a 1-0 win at Derby County.

1914 Goalkeeper James Boe conceded seven goals on his debut as Sunderland crashed 7-1 at Goodison Park. This proved to be his only game for The Lads even though contemporary match reports cleared him of blame for the defeat.

1891 Hugh Wilson became the first Sunderland player to miss a penalty; it was saved. He had earlier successfully converted a penalty in the home game against Burnley. (see September 19th)

18.11.2000

NOVEMBER 22

1975 Sunderland dropped their first home points of the season with a 1-1 draw with Bristol Rovers ending the nine game winning run. The season ended with 19 home wins and 2 draws with both Bristol clubs coming away with draws. (see March 23rd)

1969 Second half goals from Stuckey and Lathan, on his home debut, gave Sunderland a 2-2 draw with Southampton to move them off the bottom of Division One.

1958 South African Don Kichenbrand scored the first hat trick by a Sunderland player outside of the top flight; in a 4-0 win at Rotherham United. Don Revie got the other goal on his final appearance for the Black Cats.

1930 The Lads recorded their best home win over Newcastle United; 5-0 with Eden (2), Connor (2) and Gurney getting the goals.

NOVEMBER 23

1985 Eric Gates and Gary Bennett scored in a 2-1 home win over Brighton & Hove Albion.

1964 Sunderland retained top spot in Division Two after a 2-1 win at Swansea Town thanks to second half goals from Charlie Hurley and Nick Sharkey.

1951 Scottish international half back George Aitken signed from Third Lanark for £20,000.

1935 Raich Carter got both of the goals in a 2-1 home victory over Middlesbrough. It was the sixth consecutive game in which he had found the net.

(see December 7th)

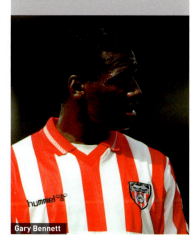
Gary Bennett

NOVEMBER 24

1990 Two goals from Marco Gabbiadini gave the Black Cats their first top flight away win of the season; 2-0 at Sheffield United.

1987 Sunderland scored seven goals in a home game for the second time that month. Rotherham United were blown away in the first half of the Freight Rover Trophy game with The Lads going in 6-1 up. The match, a 7-1 win, was unusual in that this was the first, and so far only, time that six different Sunderland players have found the net in the same game. (see November 3rd)

1984 The Sunderland v Manchester United game had everything; The Lads went 2-0 down, David Hodgson and Mark Hughes were sent off and a Clive Walker hat trick that included two penalties; all in the first 45 minutes.

1928 One of David Halliday's record twelve hat tricks for Sunderland helped them to a 5-1 victory over Manchester United at Roker Park.

NOVEMBER 25

2000 Alex Rae netted the only goal in a 1-0 win at Charlton Athletic.

1978 Two goals from Gary Rowell and one from Wayne Entwistle gave Sunderland a 3-0 win at Luton Town.

1967 Winger Bruce Stuckey made his debut at Southampton. First half goals from Ralph Brand and Neil Martin were not enough as The Lads went down 3-2.

1922 The Black Cats won 3-2 at Highbury thanks to goals from Hawes, Paterson and Donaldson to remain second in the top flight.

Alex Rae

NOVEMBER 26

1998 Midfielder Gavin McCann signed from Everton for £300,000 plus a further £200,000 based on appearances.

1993 Sunderland manager Terry Butcher was sacked with reserve team coach Mick Buxton taking over in a temporary capacity.

1966 David Herd had the unusual distinction of scoring a hat trick against three different keepers in Manchester United's 5-0 home win over Sunderland. Jim Montgomery conceded the first then went off injured; replacement keepers Charlie Hurley and John Parke then each failed to stop Herd's efforts.

1910 A 4-0 home victory over Tottenham Hotspur was Sunderland's fourteenth, and proved to be their last, unbeaten game since the start of the season and maintained their top spot in Division One.

NOVEMBER 27

2004 Substitute Michael Bridges scored the first goal of his second spell with the Club in a 1-0 win at Stoke City.

1999 Kevin Ball's substitute appearance in a 3-2 win at Watford proved to be his last game for The Lads in a career that spanned nine years. Vicarage Road old boy Kevin Phillips netted two of Sunderland's goals on his return.

1949 Birth of 1973 FA Cup winning left winger Dennis Tueart in Newcastle.

1926 Sunderland remained at the head of the top flight following a 3-0 home win over Sheffield United.

Kevin Ball

NOVEMBER 28

2000 Death of "Crown Prince of Football" Len Shackleton at the age of 78. Later that day a minute's silence was observed by a record home League Cup crowd of 47,543 who then witnessed a 2-1 victory over Manchester United.

1998 Niall Quinn scored for the sixth successive League game as The Lads convincingly won 4-0 at Sheffield United. Quinn and Bridges got two goals each.

1979 Sunderland won the Daily Express 5-a-side National Football Championship at Wembley Indoor Arena. The team of Chris Turner, Kevin Arnott, Shaun Elliott, Mick Buckley, Stan Cummins and substitute John Cooke beat Brighton 2-0 in the final following earlier wins over Ipswich Town (2-0), WBA (2-0) and Newcastle Utd (4-0).

1953 Welsh international centre forward Trevor Ford transferred to Cardiff City for £30,000.

NOVEMBER 29

1997 First half goals from Lee Clark (2) and Kevin Phillips sealed a 3-0 home victory against Tranmere Rovers.

1972 "The Messiah" arrived on Wearside. Bob Stokoe was appointed manager with caretaker manager Billy Elliott returning to his coaching duties. The first decision Stokoe made was to reintroduce the traditional black shorts, instead of white, as part of the home strip.

1947 Newbiggin born centre forward Ron Turnbull had a dream debut for Sunderland by scoring all four goals in a 4-1 home victory over Portsmouth. No other debutant has even bagged a hat trick for The Lads.

1923 Record penalty scorer Billy Clunas signed from St Mirren for £2,500.

NOVEMBER 30

1996 Two goals from substitute Michael Bridges helped Sunderland to win 3-1 at Goodison Park after coming on for the other goal scorer Craig Russell.

1976 Jimmy Adamson appointed as Sunderland's new manager taking over from caretaker manager Ian McFarlane.
(see October 16th)

1957 Sunderland beat Manchester City 2-1 at Roker Park thanks to goals from Don Revie and Stan Anderson.

1939 Death of 1913 Championship winning keeper Joseph Butler aged 60.

Jimmy Adamson

DECEMBER

DECEMBER 1

2001 Kevin Phillips scored the only goal at the Stadium of Light in a narrow victory over West Ham United.

1998 Sunderland progressed to their third League Cup semi final after a 3-0 home win over Luton Town. The game was unusual in modern times as none of the Sunderland substitutes were called upon.

1954 Len Shackleton's impudent chip over the West German keeper helped England to a 3-1 win over the World Cup holders at Wembley. This was the last time a Sunderland player scored for England.

1925 England international centre forward Robert Kelly signed from Burnley for a British record fee of £6,550.

DECEMBER 2

2003 Stewart Downing converted a penalty and Julio Arca was sent off in a 1-1 draw at home to Wigan Athletic in front of 22,167 people; the lowest League crowd at the Stadium of Light.

1978 Wayne Entwistle scored his only hat trick for The Lads in a 5-0 home win over Bristol Rovers.

1933 Patsy Gallacher achieved his second hat trick of the season in a 4-0 win at Middlesbrough.

1919 Birth of Cliff Whitelum in Farnworth, Lancashire. His best years coincided with WW2 during which time he scored over one hundred goals for the Black Cats.

Patsy Gallacher

DECEMBER 3

1995 Martin Scott's first half penalty gave Sunderland all of the points at Roker Park against Crystal Palace.

1979 Midfielder Claudio Marangoni became the first Argentinian to join Sunderland when he moved from San Lorenzo for a club record £380,000 fee. This fee was later reduced to £230,000 because he returned to South America before the end of his three year contract.

1892 Prolific centre forward John Campbell scored a hat trick in Sunderland's 5-0 win at Nottingham Forest. The "Team of all The Talents" scored five goals or more in nine of their thirty League games as they retained the League Championship with a record one hundred goals scored.

1887 Sunderland came from 2-0 down at half time to beat Middlesbrough 4-2 in their first ever FA Cup replay. However the Black Cats were disqualified from the competition for fielding three professionals; Hastings, Monaghan and Richardson in the games against Boro.

DECEMBER 4

2008 Roy Keane resigned as Sunderland manager after 100 games in charge following a run of four successive home defeats. Coach Ricky Sbragia took over the reins on a temporary basis. (see December 27th)

1999 The Stadium of Light witnessed one of its best games as a rampant Sunderland went in 4-0 up against Chelsea at half time thanks to a brace each from Quinn and Phillips.

1961 Birth of former Sunderland captain Gary Bennett in Manchester.

1909 Goals from Harry Low and George Holley (2) gave the Black Cats a 3-0 home victory over Manchester United.

04.12.1999

DECEMBER 5

1992 Michael Gray scored after only 40 seconds of his home debut as Sunderland ran out 2-1 victors over Barnsley.

1991 Centre forward Don Goodman was signed from West Bromwich Albion for a club record fee of £900,000. However he was cup tied having played in the first round for The Baggies so missed out on the run to the FA Cup final.

1984 Goals from Clive Walker and Gordon Chisholm, along with a late penalty save by Chris Turner, ensured the Black Cats 2-1 victory at White Hart Lane in a League Cup fourth round replay.

1908 It doesn't get any better than this for a Sunderland fan. The Lads scored eight times in 28 second half minutes at Newcastle United in their record 9-1 away victory. Billy Hogg and George Holley both grabbed hat tricks.

DECEMBER 6

1997 A late Niall Quinn strike gave The Lads a 1-0 victory at Loftus Road taking them back up into a Play Off position for the first time in almost three months.

1969 First half goals from Gordon Harris and Bobby Park gave the Black Cats a 2-1 victory over Ipswich Town; only their second home win of the season.

1930 Seven goals in the first half and a further four in the second provided a Roker Park crowd with plenty of entertainment as Sunderland finally emerged 6-5 winners over Liverpool.

1913 George Holley scored his eighth, and penultimate, hat trick for Sunderland in a 3-2 home win over Bolton Wanderers that took them up to third in the top flight.

DECEMBER 7

2001 USA midfielder and captain Claudio Reyna was signed from Glasgow Rangers for a Club record equalling £4.5 million. (see August 31st)

1974 Portsmouth were defeated 4-1 at Roker Park courtesy of goals from Halom, Hughes (penalty), Malone and Robson.

1935 Bobby Gurney scored five times and Raich Carter netted for the eighth consecutive game in a 7-2 home victory over Bolton Wanderers. (see February 2nd and March 20th)

1912 The Black Cats thrashed Liverpool 7-0 at Roker Park with inside forward Charlie Buchan becoming the first Sunderland player to score five goals in a League game. (see April 12th)

DECEMBER 8

2003 Stewart Downing ended his one month loan spell from Middlesbrough with the only goal in a 1-1 draw at Coventry City. The point came at a high cost to Irish midfielder Colin Healy who sustained a badly broken leg that effectively ended his Sunderland career.

1973 Sunderland beat Aston Villa 2-0 at Roker Park thanks to goals from Dennis Tueart and Vic Halom. This is one of only eight games out of more than 150 League meetings between the two clubs that have been played outside of the top flight.

1956 Charlie Fleming struck twice to give the Black Cats a 2-1 home victory over Burnley and lift them off the foot of Division One.

1888 Sunderland declined to play an FA Cup tie for the first, and only, occasion after being drawn against Sunderland Albion. The directors felt that the gate receipts from the anticipated big crowd would benefit their new rivals too much.

DECEMBER 9

1999 Former captain Kevin Ball transferred to Fulham for £200,000 after more than nine years on Wearside.

1995 Second placed Sunderland emphatically replaced Millwall at the top of Division One, thrashing them 6-0 at Roker Park. Striker Craig Russell got four after Martin Scott had opened the scoring with a penalty. Phil Gray was the other scorer.

1961 Ambrose Fogarty and Brian Clough scored hat tricks as Sunderland easily beat Swansea Town 7-2 at Roker Park.

1893 Victorian forward John Campbell scored his hundredth goal for the club in only his ninety ninth first team game; in a 3-2 home defeat to Blackburn Rovers. This was Sunderland's only home defeat between 15/09/1890 and 01/09/1896; a period of 92 League and FA Cup games.

DECEMBER 10

2004 Darren Williams moved to Cardiff City on a free transfer after more than eight years with Sunderland.

1955 First half goals from Charlie Fleming (2) and Billy Elliott sealed a 3-2 home win over Sheffield United moving The Lads up to third place in the top flight.

1952 Roker Park staged its first floodlit game. Sunderland, wearing flame coloured luminous shirts, beat Dundee 5-3 in front of a 34,352 crowd. The experiment was successful and following a few more floodlit games the temporary lights were replaced with permanent ones at the end of that season.

1921 Sunderland gained their first victory over a Welsh team as Cardiff City were beaten 4-1 at Roker Park.

DECEMBER 11

1999 The Stadium of Light staged its first FA Cup game which coincided with the earliest staging of this round since 1887. Gavin McCann's goal against Portsmouth was enough to send Sunderland through to round four.

1978 Dave Merrington resigned as caretaker manager to join up with his ex-boss Jimmy Adamson at Leeds United. (see December 13th)

1958 Ex-England international forward Ernie Taylor finally got to play for his home town club when he signed from Manchester United for £9,000 at the age of 33.

1926 David Halliday scored four times as Sunderland trounced Manchester United 6-0 at Roker Park to return to the top of Division One. Unusually all of the goals came in the second half.

11.12.1999

DECEMBER 12

1998 First half goals from Martin Smith and Paul Butler gave The Lads a 2-0 home victory over Port Vale.

1948 Birth of England defender Colin Todd in Chester-le Street.

1914 The 2-1 win against Burnley was played in front of the lowest estimated crowd for a first team game at Roker Park; only 2,000. An easterly gale, heavy showers and the start of WW1 probably accounted for this. (see April 11th)

1891 Sunderland won 7-0 at home to Darwen. They went on to beat them 7-1 in the corresponding away fixture later in the season thus recording their highest aggregate score against a team in one season. (see April 23rd)

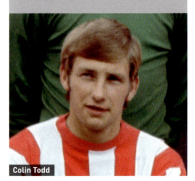

Colin Todd

DECEMBER 13

1997 Goals either side of half time from Kevin Phillips and Allan Johnston sealed a 2-0 win at the Stadium of Light against West Bromwich Albion.

1980 John Hawley picked up a loose ball and thundered a 35 yard first time shot past Arsenal's Northern Ireland keeper Pat Jennings to open the scoring in Sunderland's 2-0 home win.

1978 Former player Billy Elliott was appointed Sunderland manager for the second occasion. (see December 11th)

1975 Gary Rowell made his debut as a substitute for Mel Holden in the 1-0 home victory over Oxford United.

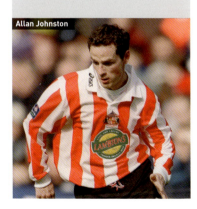
Allan Johnston

DECEMBER 14

1991 Don Goodman netted the only goal at Roker Park in the win over Leicester City.

1970 Centre forward Dave Watson signed from Rotherham United for £100,000. Caretaker manager Billy Elliott converted him into a centre half in November 1972; the position he remained in and later represented England.

1935 Future Sunderland player Ken Willingham scored the fastest goal against The Lads. He struck after only ten seconds for what turned out to be the only goal of the game at Leeds Road, Huddersfield.

1912 Sunderland continued to improve after a poor start to the season winning 4-0 at Everton thanks to goals from Richardson (2), Buchan and Mordue.

DECEMBER 15

2002 Sunderland beat Liverpool on Wearside for the first time since 1958. Goals from Gavin McCann and Michael Proctor sealed the 2-1 win. At the time the euphoric crowd could not have imagined that this would be the last home League victory of the season. (see August 30th)

1999 Irish international Kevin Kilbane signed from West Bromwich Albion for £2.5 million.

1996 A Michael Duberry own goal and second half strikes from Kevin Ball and Craig Russell gave The Lads a 3-0 win at Roker Park in front of TV cameras.

1961 Death of long serving player then manager Bill Murray aged 61.

DECEMBER 16

2006 Late goals from Grant Leadbitter and David Connolly gave the Black Cats a 2-2 draw at Turf Moor, extending their unbeaten run to seven games.

1961 Brian Clough scored for the fourth consecutive game along with a brace from Jack Overfield to give Sunderland a 3-0 home win over Walsall.

1950 Sunderland scored five times on a snow covered Baseball Ground pitch yet still lost 6-5 to Derby County.

1880 Birth of William Agnew; the first player to play for Sunderland, Newcastle United and Middlesbrough.

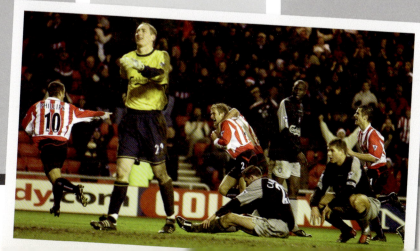
15.12.2002

DECEMBER 17

1994 Lee Howey scored twice and Gary Owers made his final appearance in Sunderland's 2-0 win over Bristol City at Roker Park. This was their 1000th League game outside of the top flight.

1960 Harry Hooper scored twice in the 3-3 draw at Swansea Town.

1949 Sunderland beat Liverpool at Roker Park thanks to goals from Tommy Wright, Len Shackleton and Harry Kirtley.

1932 Three first half goals, including a pair from Bobby Gurney, set up a 3-1 win at Portsmouth.

Gary Owers

DECEMBER 18

1999 Goals either side of half time by Kevin Phillips took his season's tally to nineteen in 18 Premiership games and gave The Lads a 2-0 home win over Southampton.

1988 The long return journey to Devon proved enjoyable as the Black Cats won 4-1 at Plymouth Argyle. Armstrong, Pascoe, Gabbiadini and Gates scored Sunderland's goals.

1982 Gary Rowell struck a hat trick in the 3-0 home win over Arsenal which lifted Sunderland off the foot of the table.

1922 Birth of Ivor Broadis in Poplar, London; who transferred himself to Sunderland in 1949 whilst player manager of Carlisle United. (see January 31st)

DECEMBER 19

1981 Barry Venison made a dramatic entrance from the substitute's bench to turn a 2-1 deficit into a 3-2 victory at Maine Road. He immediately set up Gary Rowell's 82nd minute equaliser followed five minutes later by a superb 20 yard strike to register his first Sunderland goal.

1961 Death of Sunderland's last top flight Championship winning manager John Cochrane aged 70.

1914 Tottenham Hotspur were thumped 6-0 at home by a rampant Sunderland.

1901 Birth of Sunderland's record goal scorer in a single season David Halliday in Dumfries.

DECEMBER 20

2008 Sunderland bagged their second successive four goal haul under caretaker manager Ricky Sbragia when beating Hull City 4-1 at the KC Stadium.

1997 The Black Cats won 3-0 on their first ever League visit to Crewe Alexandra courtesy of goals from Phillips, Summerbee and Quinn. The game finished in partial darkness due to floodlight failure on one side of the ground.

1947 Right back Jack Stelling got married in the morning then played in the 1-1 draw with Arsenal at Roker Park in the afternoon.

1884 Sunderland recorded their highest ever victory at any level beating Castletown 23-0 in a friendly. James Allan, one of Sunderland's founders, scored twelve of the goals.

DECEMBER 21

1986 Sunderland recorded their biggest home win of the season; 3-0 against Blackburn Rovers thanks to goals from Paul Lemon, Eric Gates and David Buchanan.

1968 Calvin Palmer and Gordon Harris were on target in the Black Cats 2-1 victory over West Ham United at Roker Park.

1945 Raich Carter transferred to Derby County for £8,000. He went on to win an FA Cup winner's medal with them in 1946 thus becoming the only player to win such medals either side of WW2.

1913 Birth of 1937 FA Cup wining captain Horatio Stratton (Raich) Carter in Hendon, Sunderland.

DECEMBER 22

2001 Claudio Reyna, on his home debut, scored the only goal of the game against manager Peter Reid's former club, Everton.

1962 Sunderland maintained second spot in Division Two with a 2-1 win over Leeds United at Roker Park.

1928 Centre forward David Halliday scored all four goals, including his only penalty for The Lads, in a 4-4 draw at home to Sheffield United.

1923 Two goals from Jock Paterson gave Sunderland a 2-0 win at Newcastle United. This completed the double over them having won 3-2 at Roker on the previous Saturday.

DECEMBER 23

2000 Sunderland beat Manchester City 1-0 at the Stadium of Light thanks to a first half goal from Don Hutchison.

1994 Left back Martin Scott signed from Bristol City in a deal worth £750,000 (£450,000 plus Gary Owers moving in the other direction).

1950 The Black Cats ended a spell of only one win in eleven games with a 2-1 home victory over Liverpool.

1899 Centre forward Robert Hogg scored the first League hat trick by a Sunderland player against Newcastle United in a 4-2 win at St James' Park.

DECEMBER 24

1996 Sunderland AFC was floated on the London stock market with shares valued at 585p. The two million and fifty thousand shares on offer immediately rose in value and opened at 732p each.

1938 John Spuhler scored the only goal of the game, his penultimate one for The Lads, to beat Birmingham at Roker Park.

1921 Debutant Arthur "Tricky" Hawes scored twice in a 5-0 demolition of West Bromwich Albion at Roker Park.

1904 After seven attempts Sunderland finally beat Newcastle United on Wearside in a League game. The 3-1 win included goals from Harry Buckle, Richard Jackson and an own goal by former Sunderland player Andy McCombie.

Raich Carter

DECEMBER 25

1956 Sunderland beat Aston Villa 1-0 at Roker Park in their last ever Christmas Day game. Northern Ireland international winger Billy Bingham scored the only goal.

1953 Centre half Fred Hall scored his only goal for The Lads in 224 appearances in a 1-1 draw at home to Huddersfield Town.

1950 Goals either side of half time by Tommy Wright sealed a 2-1 home victory over Manchester United.

1914 Surely the best Christmas present for any Sunderland fan. The Black Cats won 5-2 at St James' Park courtesy of a Bobby Best hat trick and one each from inside forwards Charlie Buchan and George Philip.

DECEMBER 26

2000 A Kevin Phillips hat trick helped seal a 4-1 win at Bradford City to take Sunderland up to third in the Premiership.

1962 Centre forward Brian Clough was averaging a goal a game until he suffered a cruciate ligament injury in the home game against Bury that ended his season. This injury ultimately ended his career at the age of 29.
(see September 2nd)

1934 The Black Cats chewed up The Toffees 7-0 at Roker Park, only twenty four hours after losing 6-2 to Everton at Goodison Park, to return to the top of Division One.

1911 Sunderland went in 7-0 down at half time at Sheffield Wednesday and ultimately lost by a club record 8-0.
(see September 25th and October 19th)

Brian Clough

DECEMBER 27

2008 Ricky Sbragia appointed manager of Sunderland after 23 days in temporary charge following the resignation of Roy Keane.

1983 A `Pop' Robson goal and a rare "brace from Brace" (Paul Bracewell) gave The Lads a 3-0 home win over West Bromwich Albion.

1957 Full back, and later Sunderland manager, Len Ashurst signed from Prescot Cables on part time forms (to allow him to complete his apprenticeship as a printer).

1952 Sunderland moved to third place in the top flight with a 5-2 win over Wolverhampton Wanderers at Roker Park.

DECEMBER 28

1999 Sunderland rocked table topping Manchester United by going 2-0 up after only twelve minutes through McCann and Quinn. Roy Keane then put in one of the most influential performances by an away player at the Stadium of Light to drag United back into the game and eventually gain a 2-2 draw in front of 42,026 – a new stadium record crowd which included the then Prime Minister Tony Blair.

1998 Crewe Alexandra were beaten 2-0 at the Stadium of Light by goals from Danny Dichio and substitute Michael Bridges.

1963 First half goals from George Herd and Nick Sharkey sunk table topping Leeds United 2-0 at Roker Park and kept Sunderland in second spot in Division Two.

1935 Sunderland beat League Champions Arsenal 5-4 at Roker Park to remain on the top of the table and on course to take over the title that The Gunners had held for the previous three seasons.

111

DECEMBER 29

1988 Welsh international goalkeeper Tony Norman signed from Hull City in a deal valued at £450,000 (The Tigers received Iain Hesford, Billy Whitehurst and £220,000).

1979 Claudio Marangoni's second of only three goals he scored for The Lads was a 25 yard thunderbolt in a 1-0 win at Fulham.

1967 FA Cup final goal scoring hero Ian Porterfield signed from Raith Rovers for £45,000.

1951 Arsenal lost 4-1 at Roker Park as a result of strikes from international forwards Shackleton, Ford (2) and Bingham.

Tony Norman

DECEMBER 30

2000 A second half recovery at Highbury with goals from Phillips (penalty) and McCann saw The Lads gain a point having trailed 2-0 at half time.

1991 Assistant manager Malcolm Crosby replaced the sacked Denis Smith. He made an immediate impact winning all four games in January, gaining that month's Manager of the Month award and steering Sunderland to a Wembley FA Cup final against Liverpool.

1967 Two first half goals from Colin Suggett, on his nineteenth birthday, and one just after the break from Bruce Stuckey gave the Black Cats a 3-3 draw with Newcastle United at Roker Park in one of their best performances of the season.

1961 The home game against Charlton Athletic became the first match to be postponed at Roker Park since Christmas Day 1925.

30.12.2000

DECEMBER 31

1988 Debutant keeper Tony Norman started with a clean sheet as Sunderland finished the year with a convincing 4-0 win over Portsmouth thanks to goals from Gates, Ord, Armstrong and Pascoe.

1976 Mick Docherty signed from Manchester City for £10,000 and was immediately appointed club captain by Jimmy Adamson.
(see January 3rd)

1966 Manchester City were defeated at Roker Park by debutant Bobby Kerr's first goal for the club.

1960 Six second half goals took Sunderland to a 7-1 home victory over Luton Town. Jimmy Davison replaced outside right Harry Hooper in the only team change manager Alan Brown made in eleven consecutive games.